THE BOOK OF KELLS

FORTY-EIGHT PAGES AND DETAILS
IN COLOUR FROM
THE MANUSCRIPT IN TRINITY
COLLEGE, DUBLIN

SELECTED AND INTRODUCED BY
PETER BROWN
Librarian of Trinity College,
Dublin

 THAMES AND HUDSON

Photography by John Kennedy of The Green
Studio, Dublin
Filmset in Great Britain by Keyspools Ltd.
Golborne, Lancashire
Printed and bound in the Netherlands by
Smeets B.V. Weert

Contents

Captions to the plates

JOHN

Introduction to the Book of Kells

THE MOST famous manuscript in the Library of Trinity College Dublin is the Book of Kells, the most sumptuous of the books to have survived from Europe's early Middle Ages. Its Latin text of the four Gospels, written in majestic lines of the most beautiful Insular majuscule script, is accompanied not only by large lavishly painted illuminated pages with intricate shapes and patterns but also by brilliant decorations within the lines of the text itself, so that only two of its 680 pages (340 folios) are without colour. The Book of Kells has not survived completely intact, and originally had about 370 folios; some of the Preliminaries before the Gospels are missing and St John's Gospel breaks off in the middle of the 17th chapter. It is a very large book both in the number and in the size of the pages, which on average measure 33 cm × 24 cm (13 in. × $9\frac{1}{2}$ in.). This magnificent book was not made for daily use or study. It was a sacred work of art, produced 1,200 years ago as a dazzling decoration presumably to appear at the altar for very special occasions.

The origins of the Book of Kells are shrouded in uncertainty. Although it has some features that link it with 8th-century Ireland, there are other elements that point to the early Church in Northumbria. Its text of the Gospels is a mixture, long retained by the Irish Church, of the Vulgate with many words and phrases from the earlier Old Latin translation of the Bible. The sources of its illustration and decoration seem to be many: from Ireland, from the Anglo-Saxons, from the continent and perhaps beyond. Where and how all these traditions and influences came together in the Book of Kells poses a problem that still remains to be fully solved. But these questions apply to other manuscripts as well, and it would be wrong to consider the Book of Kells as an isolated phenomenon. Some of the evidence has to be sought particularly in a group of manuscripts (in which there are some similar features of text, of script and of illustration) belonging to the group of islands off the west coast of the European continent and, therefore, given the name Insular. What has survived represents only a very small part of the books produced by the monasteries in these islands. The Scandinavian raids of the 9th century destroyed the majority of what must have existed. But there are also other sources of evidence in the fields of archaeology and art history, and perhaps it is from these that we have to look for further information and guidance.

I have aimed, in the brief text that accompanies the reproductions, to give some picture of the various elements that led to the Book of Kells being produced, going back to the early centuries of our era, to trace the foundations for the Latin text, and to those diverse developments of the Christian Church in Celtic Britain, Ireland and

Anglo-Saxon England which produced the monastic communities, their libraries and scriptoria.

I have not attempted to do more than provide a framework. The details are technical and the sources for them are given in the brief reading list that I have added. Above all I have not attempted to trace the origin of those aspects and elements of the decoration that are so fully described by Mlle Henry in her study of the manuscript in the 1974 publication of reproductions. I have restricted my guidance to telling the reader what he should look for as he studies the decoration of the pages in the Book of Kells.

The colour plates show reproductions of selected pages from the Book of Kells reduced from the average manuscript page size of 33 cm × 24 cm (13 in. × $9\frac{1}{2}$ in.) to an average page size of 23.4 cm × 17 cm (9 in. × $6\frac{1}{2}$ in.). The pages in this volume are, therefore, only about two-thirds the size of the large manuscript pages.

On the other hand, the enlargements that have been placed facing some of the illuminated pages, so that the minute features of the decoration may be clearly seen, are larger than the manuscript itself, some showing the details at twice their actual size.

The contrast in the size between the illuminated pages and the enlarged details facing them leads inevitably to the colours producing a different visual effect.

The pages selected for the plates have been kept in the order of the folios in the manuscript, but it has not been possible to retain in every instance the recto (R) or verso (V) side of folios in their correct position. But some pages facing each other in the manuscript have retained their position in the plates: 2V and 3R, 7V and 8R, 32V and 33R.

Captions to the plates are on page 4

NATIVITAS XPI IN BETHLEM IUDE MAGI MUNERA OFFERUNT
ET INFANTES INTERFICIUNTUR

 matheus

ꝺꝛessicutpꝛimus poin
tuꝛ inoꝛdine :· · :

ꝺuueuangelium mucha. pꝛimus sꝛipsit cuis
uocauo uuꝺnin expuplicauis uuubus fuit
ꝺuoꝛum inʒeneꝛauohe xꝑi pꝛincipia pꝛɑe

hannisharu z uuh.............uie

hic supeꝛcum spsci ꝍpniꝺns piꝺeseꝛio
temptauus :· ꝍpostyuumtauuutis est ioha
huspꝛuuchaueuuhis euuocaui ꝺisapulos ꝍ

18

Phatuir tesamonium puanba eleopo dicit
non sum dignus corrigian calciamenti
eius soluere ... Item iohannis dicit ecce
agnus dei qui tollit peccatum mundi ..
Ostendit ihs discipulis suis ubi manere ... et
secutus sunt eum · Ubi ihs deaqua uinum fecit
Inchanna galilae ... Eiecit ihs eltemplo om
nes uendentes dixit domus orationis est
domus patris mei · Quinon renatus fuerit denouo
exaqua et spū sco non intrabit in regnum di ...
Ubi baptizat ihs dixit iohannis discipulis
ego non sum xps · Ubi secessit ihs aiudea et
abiit in samariam ... peter bible erch
Sedens super puteum mulierem samaritanam
et discipulis suis alii laborauerunt et uos inla
borem ipsorum introistis · Omnis propheta sine
honore est in patria est · suscitabit filium reguli sana
uit ...
· 24 ·

1 The continental background of Latin and learning

ON CHRISTMAS DAY in the year 800, as Charlemagne, King of the Franks, knelt in St Peter's in Rome to hear Pope Leo III celebrate the Christmas mass, the Pope approached and unexpectedly (so it was said) crowned Charlemagne with a diadem amid public acclaim: 'Carolo augusto a Deo coronato, magno et pacifico imperatore, vita et victoria.'

With this significant action, marking the official beginning of a new Roman empire with a Christian emperor of Latin Christendom, formal recognition was given to the dramatic changes that Charlemagne, with the Northumbrian scholar Alcuin from York, had begun to introduce in 782 in the Frankish court at Aix. The changes were to give a new direction to the political, as well as to the religious and cultural, life of the European continent and eventually these effects were to be felt even in the islands at the far western edge of Europe. At the time, however, these islands were themselves little affected by such stirring developments, great as their own contribution had been to both the religious and the cultural scene in Europe over the previous two hundred years, great as their direct contribution now was to the achievements of the Carolingian renaissance in Europe.

For the Carolingians drew their impetus, their scholarship, their expertise and their traditions less from pagan Rome itself than from the reflection of pagan Rome in all the developments of the Roman Church: education and scholarship, Latin and learning during the Dark Ages and the early Middle Ages. Many of these were transferred from the continent to the western islands of Britain and Ireland and were then returned to the continent and to the Carolingians, transformed and enriched.

It was during the early years of the Carolingian educational and scholarly developments, in the last quarter of the 8th century, that the labours of writing, drawing and painting were undertaken that created the Book of Kells. But the expertise and traditions that produced the Book of Kells were not elements of that Carolingian world. They formed a part of the complexity of relationships and developments that the Carolingian renaissance drew upon, a complexity that can be traced further and further backwards in time.

The tumultuous period from the first westward advances of the Huns under Attila, in 375, until the decline of the Ostrogothic rulers of Rome, in the middle of the 6th century, was also the period in which the impact of Roman classical culture upon the Middle Ages was founded. It was a linguistic rather than a literary impact and was based on the way in which Latin was used, both grammatically and stylistically.

The origins for this are to be found in Rome even earlier, in the middle of the 4th century, in the teaching of Aelius Donatus, a Roman grammarian and rhetorician, whose *Ars minor* gave elementary instruction in the eight parts of speech, while his *Ars major* also provided the elements of grammar and correct grammatical use of Latin with examples drawn from classical writers, particularly Cicero and Virgil, and from a variety of later Roman writers. This was to be used as a manual for the learning of Latin during the next eight hundred years.

But of even greater significance was the tuition that St Jerome received as a young boy in Rome in the early 360s from Aelius Donatus. Although later in life Jerome deliberately rejected classical Roman literature as a reflection of the pagan world and therefore unsuitable for a Christian, his own usage of Latin was greatly influenced by the extensive knowledge of classical Latin literature that he had gained in his earlier education.

In the year 382, Pope Damasus commissioned Jerome, as an outstanding biblical scholar with adequate knowledge of both Greek and Hebrew, to undertake an improved Latin translation of the Bible. A Latin translation of the Bible was known as early as the latter part of the 2nd century in the Roman province in Africa, where Latin was the vernacular language. By the early 3rd century there were several versions of this Latin translation in Rome and by the latter part of the 4th century the Old Latin Bible was an unedifying mixture of textual confusion with both colloquial and erroneous Latin. St Jerome's task was to edit this with revised translation into a new version.

A large part of the new version – the *editio vulgata* – was the work of St Jerome, and his revised translation of the Gospels formed an early part of his contribution. The Vulgate was commonly accepted in place of the Old Latin version throughout most of Europe by the end of the 6th century (although we shall see the reluctance of the Celtic Church to change to the new text). However, it was not until the Council of Trent, in 1546, that the Vulgate became the authoritative text of the Latin Bible and only in 1592 was the revised version of Pope Clement VIII officially accepted by the Roman Church.

A second manual followed shortly after that of Aelius Donatus, which was to have an even greater effect on the schools of the Middle Ages and, therefore, on the knowledge and use of the Latin language. This was the treatise *De nuptiis Philologiae et Mercurii* by Martianus Capella, who taught and practised in the law courts at Carthage in the early 5th century. In the form of an allegory, the seven fields of knowledge are described by the seven bridesmaids to Philologia at her wedding to Mercury. The discourse of the seven maidens (Grammar, Rhetoric, Dialectic, Geometry, Arithmetic, Astronomy and Music) provided a textbook for Latin and education in not only the 5th century, but the whole of the Middle Ages and beyond. The liberal arts were a concept of education that came from the classical Romans: Cicero had included medicine and law, but Varro did not and, following him, Martianus Capella fixed the number of liberal arts at seven. Moreover, the examples he provided for both Grammar and Rhetoric were taken solely from the literature of pagan Rome, and these were to be the models on which the education of the Christian community was founded throughout the Middle Ages.

More than a hundred years after Martianus, about the year 540, a far more authoritative voice set out clearly the two principles that were to form the foundations of the developing education and culture of medieval Europe: the preservation of classical language, learning and culture in the new age, and the establishment of monastic life as the context in which this culture should be nurtured. This was the voice of Cassiodorus, scholar minister to the first Ostrogothic ruler over Rome, Theodoric the Great. It is a reflection of the great gulf in understanding and interest between the Middle Ages and the modern world that two ministers to Theodoric, Boethius author of the 'best seller' of the Middle Ages *De consolatione Philosophiae*, and Cassiodorus author of the *Institutiones*, both widely known and influential writers for almost a thousand years, should now be so little known.

The shock to the patrician families of Rome and to the provincials of having to live under a barbarian regime led to doubts of the survival of Roman Latin culture and tradition. Strictly speaking, Theodoric was king only of the Ostrogoths in Italy and his position in Rome was that of Praetorian Prefect and a servant of Zeno, the last emperor at Constantinople of East and West. The whole fabric of Roman administration and the late imperial offices were maintained as far as possible, and Cassiodorus as *magister officiorum* at the Gothic court at Ravenna headed this administration. It became increasingly clear, however, that conflicts between the Eastern emperors and the West, between Aryan and Catholic Christianity, between the Gothic rulers and the Roman senate, between Byzantine and Roman cultures in a period of Roman decline–all posed a serious threat to the survival of *Romanitas*. At the end of a career in which he had tried to maintain the public system of imperial Rome, Cassiodorus designed the system for the preservation of classical Latin and Roman learning through the establishment of the monastic school. At the city of Squillace, by the Ionian Sea, Cassiodorus established his monastery, Vivarium.

The ideal of the isolated monastic life had only recently reached Western Europe from the East, and particularly from Egypt, based on the desire to follow the hermit life of the desert fathers. By 410 in Gaul, St Honoratus had already founded an isolated monastery on the Mediterranean island of Lérins where the monks could seek spiritual perfection. St Martin had founded his monastery near Tours. In Italy, Cassiodorus's contemporary, Benedict of Nursia, began to live as a hermit in a cave in the cliff of Subiaco in the foothills of the Apennines. He attracted followers and the hermit monastery of Subiaco was built, followed by St Benedict's greatest monastery, Monte Casino, where he formulated the monastic daily timetable and the *sancta regula*, the Benedictine Rule for the government, well-being and regulation of the monastery community.

In his monastic community at Squillace, Cassiodorus introduced two institutions, which together ensured the survival and widespread knowledge of classical Latin culture and at the same time gave to Latin Christianity a scholarly basis for its theology, its liturgy and its interpretation of the Bible. These two institutions, the monastic school and the scriptorium, were to play a predominant part in many of the monasteries that were established throughout Europe during the coming centuries. And it was on these two institutions that the Carolingian religious and cultural developments were eventually based.

The Roman *scholae publicae* had not survived in Gaul and Britain after the collapse of the empire in the early years of the 5th century, and although they continued to exist in Italy during the Ostrogothic regime they were in a state of decline and ceased by the middle of the 6th century. These schools had been provided freely over centuries to provide an adequate supply of educated boys for Roman public service. The *rhetors* who instructed the boys had taught them the liberal arts so that they should be literate, numerate and able to make full use of classical learning and literature.

It was to maintain and restore this system of education that Cassiodorus introduced the monastic school, but designed to prepare boys for the religious life instead of public service. Education was always a preparation for an ecclesiastical life and was provided on a personal basis by a bishop, or at a school in a monastery. There were no schools for lay pupils, although an abbot would sometimes accept a lay boy in his monastic school.

The courses of instruction that Cassiodorus laid out in his *Institutiones* prescribed a wide variety of reading, with over a hundred authors. For ecclesiastical reading, apart from the books of the Bible and the works of Christian authors, St Ambrose, St Augustine of Hippo and St Jerome, he included the historians, Livy, Orosius, Rufinus and Prosper of Aquitaine. For reading the Gospels, he explained the use of the Eusebian Canon Tables.

For secular reading, he included a wide variety of Latin authors and recommended the guidance of Aelius Donatus, but he also showed his own particular preference for Cicero and Virgil. By the end of the 6th century, attitudes had changed and Pope Gregory the Great scorned pagan classical literature as a basis for Christian education and learning, allowing only the texts and literature of the Bible and the Church. This attitude was not held universally, and certainly not so strongly, but it continued to influence monastic scholars until the Carolingians included comprehensively all pagan as well as Christian literature as sources for learning.

Cassiodorus was a capable scholar and understood the need for a great library of books for both religious and secular studies. To achieve this he not only brought many books to his monastery, Vivarium, but he set up in the monastery a scriptorium to make copies of books as a means of preserving the writings of both classical and Christian authors. It was on the basis of the availability of such copies that Cassiodorus could list and comment on the writings of so many authors in his *Institutiones*. For, although some of the works of a few of the acknowledged greatest Roman writers, Virgil, Ovid, Cicero, existed in copies written on vellum, other works of the greatest

Roman writers and all the surviving works of writers of lesser reputation existed only on deteriorating papyrus copies. The widespread copying of books onto vellum as a means of preserving ancient texts had to await the dynamism of the Carolingians 150 years later, but the example of the Vivarium scriptorium was to be followed increasingly throughout European monasteries.

Vivarium produced not only copies of the writings of earlier authors, but also a number of textual works resulting from the scholarly tradition that Cassiodorus had established. Among these was a text of the Vulgate revised by Cassiodorus in nine volumes, with some books of the Bible divided into chapters and written out as a *codex grandior littera clariore conscriptus*. The Codex Amiatinus, a copy of the Gospels written at Jarrow in Northumbria in the 8th century, is believed to have been copied from a copy of the text by Cassiodorus, and a painting at the beginning of the Codex shows a bookshelf on which a Bible in nine volumes stands clearly labelled. This Codex Amiatinus is one of the copies of the Gospels that must be considered alongside the Book of Kells.

At the end of the 6th century, a new and very different influence was felt on the continent. Monasteries were founded that laid great emphasis on the developments already seen at Vivarium: the monastic school and the scriptorium. This new impetus originated in Ireland and, soon after the year 590, brought to the continent a number of the features that had developed in the Irish Church during its long and unbroken development over 150 years. In this respect Ireland was very different from most other parts of Europe, where Christianity had been only partly sustained, interrupted by periods of return to paganism. More than anything else, the invasions of the pagan Germanic tribes, the Franks and Burgundians in Gaul, the Angles and Saxons in Britain, had weakened or destroyed the Christian organization of the peoples they had overwhelmed. The Irish Church at the end of the 6th century was monastic in outlook and was already missionary, having undertaken a mission to the Picts in Scotland. In 591, an evangelic mission to the continent was headed by St Columbanus, who set out from the Irish monastery of Bangor with a band of companions for the Merovingian kingdom in France.

Many Franks were already largely Christian (the religion they had absorbed from the Gauls), but their Christian faith was not strong and, not infrequently, Christian practices were neglected or even replaced by pagan rites. Columbanus was at first well received and soon founded his first significant monastery at Luxeuil, setting it up in the Irish tradition. The Irish Church had several features, however, that did not conform with the practices of the continental Catholic Church. As they had no territorial bishops of their own, they disregarded the diocesan bishops on the continent. Moreover, the method of dating Easter, adhered to by the Celtic Church (but no longer used by any other part of the Catholic Church), and the Irish form of tonsure, in which only the front of the head was shaven, made them clearly different from the bishops and priests of the continent. After some ten years, opposition forced the Irish monks to move on southward up the Rhine to Lake Constance, where the Alemanni had relapsed into paganism. There Columbanus and his monks remained for three years preaching Christianity, but then were again forced to move on. One of the monks, Gallus, was prevented by illness from travelling, and when he recovered he established a hermitage in the mountains. His fame spread and after his death the hermitage developed into a cell for anchorite monks, a place of pilgrimage. In 720, the cell developed into an abbey and soon began to lose its Irish features and the Columban organization of the monastic community. The Irish Church prescribed reading for the monks, and books were collected at St Gall from an early date, some of the *Libri scottice scripti* (as they are described in the old catalogue) possibly having been brought from Ireland by Irish monks during the 7th and 8th centuries. In addition to these, the St Gall Gospels, completed about the year 800, have to be considered as an example of the Irish illuminative art that we find in the Book of Kells.

The monastic school at St Gall was not founded until 720, when the school and the scriptorium began to produce scribes, scholars and books in such numbers that by the 9th century St Gall was famous throughout Europe for its learning. Following the few Irish monks of the early missionary period in the 7th century, many more arrived in the floodtide of Irish influence on the continent during the 9th century. But by then St Gall had lost its Irish elements, and since the middle of the 8th century had been governed by the Benedictine Rule.

After leaving Gallus behind, Columbanus travelled with his companions south to the far side of the Alps, and founded, in 613, a monastery at the remote site of Bobbio. It, too, became a centre for scholarship, and a large library was built up (partly by exchange of copies with St Gall and Luxeuil). From its scriptorium a large number of copies of books was produced that retained Irish traditions.

In the 8th and 9th centuries, Irish missionaries travelled widely on the continent and many monasteries were founded with Irish associates. These monasteries, like those in Ireland, were esteemed for their schools at which Latin and learning were so highly cultivated. The Irish influence had already begun on the continent while the Angles and Saxons in Britain were still pagan, before the first mission to them was sent by Pope Gregory the Great and before Irish monks founded monasteries in Northumbria. However, both the Roman Church and the Irish Church in England were, in little more than a century, to produce results that would have far-reaching consequences in England and on the continent. After the establishment from Rome of the first episcopal see in England at Canterbury, its influence did not extend beyond Kent for a long time. Conversion to Christianity among Angles and Saxons was carried out mainly by Irish missionaries.

From Devon in the west of England, an area then still largely pagan, came St Boniface, who in 716 travelled as a missionary to the continent to convert the heathen in many parts of Europe, from Frisia to Bavaria, and to reform the irregularities of the Frankish Church. But it was in the area of Germany that he was to make the greatest impact, founding many monasteries, the most famous at Fulda, all with the Benedictine Rule and with much emphasis on scholarship and the need for books and schools. St Boniface followed the practice of the Roman Church and organized monasteries and churches within the jurisdiction of bishops, thereby hastening the change of the continental Irish monasteries to Benedictine and Roman conformity. He was killed by pagans at Dokkum in the year 755. As a scholar, St Boniface related closely to Bede and Northumbria, where two traditions of education and scholarship had combined: the tradition of Celtic Latinity, transmitted through Aidan's Columban community at Lindisfarne, and the tradition of Anglo-Saxon learning, transmitted directly from Rome through Canterbury and through Benedict Biscop, the founder of Bede's monastery at Jarrow.

Northumbria also produced the man who, with the support and influence of Charlemagne, was to make the greatest impact of all throughout the continent. This was Alcuin from York, who joined Charlemagne's Frankish court at Aix in 782 and brought to full fruition all those elements of Latin and learning that had been developing over the centuries. He organized the development of cathedral and monastic schools, for the clerks as well as for the monks, and reinforced the basis of education inherited from Aelius Donatus, Martianus Capella and Cassiodorus: the seven liberal arts, the *Trivium* of Grammar, Rhetoric and Dialetic, the *Quadrivium* of Geometry, Arithmetic, Astronomy and Music. To the Carolingians, Grammar was at the root of all education, for it ensured the proper understanding and use of Latin. They had no reservations about pagan writers as authorities and models, with Virgil, Ovid and Cicero as the most popular, but they equally valued the Christian authors, St Augustine of Hippo, Boethius and Bede. Education to a basic level flourished, as well as scholarship and textual commentary to a higher level. This scholastic activity was necessarily accompanied by an increase in the production of books in the monastic scriptoria, where scribes laboured to make many copies to meet the demand for the more popular texts, or to make additional copies of documents and correspondence, and also copied onto vellum the many classical Latin works that had survived only precariously on the ridged and brittle surface of papyrus.

Many of the decisive factors, both physically and culturally, that made this Carolingian development possible lie in the activities that had taken place over many centuries in Britain and Ireland.

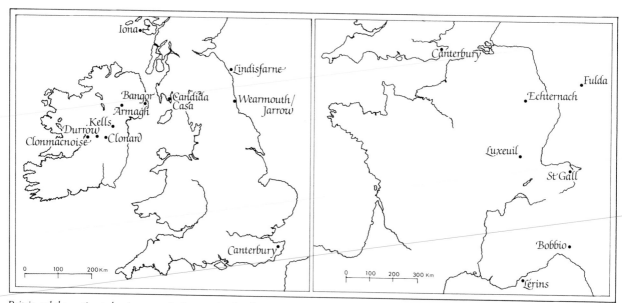

Britain and the continent showing monastic sites mentioned in the text

II The island traditions

IN THE LATE Roman Empire and the early Middle Ages the British Isles proved to be the meeting-point at which a number of contrasting traditions came into contact. In some instances this contact led to conflict in which one tradition became dominant at the expense of another. In other cases contact between two traditions led to the emergence of something new to which both earlier traditions had contributed.

The various elements that can be traced as having contributed to the Book of Kells represent both kinds of contact, and much of the history of the contrasting traditions lies in the differing ways in which Christianity came to the various parts of the islands and in the ways in which a Christian community developed.

The Celtic Britons, through the Roman population in Britain, had experienced conversion to Christianity since the 2nd century. In spite of the disruptions of the 3rd-century persecutions of Diocletian, the Christian Catholic Church had become organized and numerically powerful in the islands of Britain by the time of the final departure of the Roman legions in the early years of the 5th century. But, thereafter, the harassing raids from the Picts of Scotland and the Scots of Ireland caused increasing damage to the Britons, no longer protected by Romans. The only threat to the British Church came from the spread of the heresy of the Briton, Pelagius, who maintained that man could attain perfection by his own efforts without requiring God's grace. The Britons sought assistance from the Church in Gaul, and Bishop Germanus of Auxerre was sent in 429 and again in 447 to banish the heretic teachers and to strengthen the Catholic Church that now seemed likely to prosper among the Britons for a long time to come.

However, not only the British Church but the whole future survival of the Britons was endangered within a few years as a result of a disaster that the Britons brought upon themselves. Bede, the Northumbrian scholar writing three centuries later, describes their doom:

> Therefore, not long afterwards an even harsher retribution overtook this sinful nation for its wicked crimes. A council was held on what should be done and where protection should be sought to prevent or to repel the fierce and frequent raids of the northern races. It was agreed together with their King Vortigern that they should call to their aid the Saxons from across the sea. As the consequences clearly showed, their decision was ordained by God so that disaster should come to them for their wickedness. (Bede. *Ecclesiastical History of the English People* Bk I ch. 14.)

The Angles, the Saxons and the Jutes came by invitation in three longships in the year

449, but it soon became evident that they regarded Britain as a land to be seized. A larger fleet, with a greater body of warriors, came over from the continent, devastating the land and destroying the buildings and churches of the Britons. The Britons themselves were massacred in large numbers, among them many of their Christian priests and bishops. Some survivors managed to flee to the hills in the west and north, or even overseas, while those who surrendered were doomed to lifelong slavery. Following the Germanic warriors, hordes of Anglian and Saxon settlers came from their north European homelands and established themselves in Britain, alien and pagan.

Slowly, the defeated Britons recovered their strength, emerged from their hiding places in the more remote areas of Britain and made repeated challenges against their conquerors. But, again, the Britons brought failure upon themselves, for those who had survived the battles with the foreign enemy now attacked each other. Their own historian, Gildas of St David's in Wales, recorded with sorrow their many crimes but above all reproached the Britons that they had refused to preach the Christian faith to the Saxons.

By the end of the 6th century, the Angles and Saxons were in possession of most of the land that can now be called England, and the Celtic Britons with their Celtic Church lived only in the remote areas in the west. The greater part of the island was once more pagan.

But already Christianity had found a new foothold among the Germanic kingdoms in England, the impetus having come not from Britain, nor from Christian Ireland, but from Rome. In the year 596, Pope Gregory the Great, the eminent scholar and administrator of the Church, sent Augustine with a band of thirty monks to preach the word of God to the barbarous Angles and Saxons. The missionaries arrived in Kent and made many conversions, establishing at Canterbury an abbey and the episcopal see. The Church of the English was in this way added to the Roman patriarchate, with far-reaching consequences not only in England but on the continent in the ensuing centuries.

Before following further the developments among the Anglo-Saxons, we must look back again to the beginning of another separate tradition, in the period when Britain was still a province of the Roman Empire and Christianity was a powerful force among the Britons.

There is no direct evidence of any Christian community in Ireland at the beginning of the 5th century, but some Christians must have existed because, by 431, Pope Celestine I considered it necessary to send to those Scots (i.e. Irishmen) who believed in Christ their first bishop, Palladius. The Christian community in Ireland was to change rapidly and dramatically, not through the activities of Bishop Palladius, apparently, but as the result of a dedicated mission to Ireland by St Patrick.

There is no clear single account of the life of St Patrick, and the tangle of traditions and legends provides little that can be regarded as entirely reliable. St Patrick's own narrative of his life and of his mission to Ireland is contained in his *Confessio* and tells how as a boy he was seized by Irish raiders from his noble family's Roman estate and carried off with many other Britons to remote Ireland where for six years he tended sheep. He escaped and found passage on a ship, not back to Britain but apparently to Gaul. (A later tradition describes his travels through Gaul to the Mediterranean to the monastery on the island of Lérins.) Some years afterwards he returned to his home in Britain, but in a vision he received a letter headed 'The Voice of the people of Ireland' which begged him to return to them. He took this to be an instruction from God to go to Ireland to convert the heathen to Christianity. Once again Patrick left his home in Britain for Ireland, it is said in the year 432. Meeting no opposition from the Irish kings, St Patrick established churches with bishops and priests, founding the metropolitan church at Armagh in 444.

It must be remembered that at the time of St Patrick's success in Ireland, the Church of his own countrymen in Britain was soon to be shattered by the pagan Angles and Saxons. In contrast, the Irish Church was to remain stable and unthreatened for centuries, though not without change.

The organization established in Ireland by St Patrick was that normally found in Catholic Britain and Gaul, with a structure of archbishops, bishops and priests in charge of the churches, and with an orthodox basis of Latin Roman Christianity. The 8th-century Catalogue of the Saints of Ireland gives a picture of this organization:

> The first order of Catholic saints was in the time of Patrick; and then the founders of the churches were all bishops, 350 in number, famed and holy and full of the Holy Ghost. They had one head, Christ. They had one leader, Patrick, they maintained one mass, one liturgy, one tonsure from ear to ear. They celebrated one Easter on the fourteenth moon after the vernal equinox, and what was excommunicated by one church was excommunicated by all. They did not disapprove the assistance and participation of women since, founded on the rock of Christ, they feared not the wind of temptation. This order of saints lasted for four reigns. ... All these bishops had come from the Romans and Franks and Britons and Scots. (Translated from *Catalogus SS. Hib.*, Hadden & Stubbs.)

In many respects the Irish Church proved to be extremely traditional and conservative. The matters of the tonsure and the calculation of Easter were to bring it into direct conflict with the Catholic Church of Rome in the following centuries. In other respects, however, the Irish Church was more than ready to accept new features that were to bring about a transformation in its way of life and activities, the new features of monasticism and evangelistic missionary zeal.

The conventional style of ecclesiastical organization introduced by St Patrick did not last long. After only fifty years Armagh had ceased to be the metropolitan centre of the Irish Church and had become a monastery, while at Kildare St Brigid had founded a large community for monks and nuns. Rapidly, other churches were changed into monasteries, or new monastic centres were founded, at Clonard, Clonmacnoise, Durrow, Bangor and widely throughout the island. A hundred years later, by the end of the 6th century, the transformation was complete and the administration and organization of the Church were no longer territorial, under the jurisdiction of bishops. Instead, there were monasteries scattered throughout Ireland, each under the control of an independent abbot and acting as the religious centre for the area. There were still bishops to perform ceremonies, but they were merely part of the monastic community and subject to the head of the monastery.

The Irish Christians founded their monasteries not only in populated areas. They emulated the primitive asceticism of the hermits of the Holy Land and Egypt, who had deliberately left the populated areas to build their isolated cells in the desert where they sought perfection through prayer and fasting.

For the Irish monks, this isolation was to be found in the remote islands in the middle of lakes or off the coast of Ireland, and already by the beginning of the 6th century they were beginning to seek self-imposed exile on these island sanctuaries. The most extreme of these sites were no more than pinnacles of rock rising above the sea, but more usually the settlements consisted of a number of small buildings surrounded by fields, where the monastic community could support itself independently. This community not only had to provide for its own daily needs, but had to have among its members all the craftsmen needed to produce and maintain buildings and equipment. In addition to these requirements a monastery needed at least a few books for liturgical use, for the education of the younger members of the community in Latin and for scholarly study in those monasteries where learning was cultivated.

Little has survived in Ireland to give a clear picture of their schools and scholarship in the 6th and 7th centuries. But the high quality of both religious and classical education and study in the Irish monasteries can be recognized from the scholarly achievements of those monks who left to undertake missions in other countries.

The earliest of these missionaries was St Columba, whose departure, about 563, to preach the word of God to the Picts in northern Scotland was to have resounding consequences. Columba had already founded a number of monasteries in Ireland: the most important was the monastery of Durrow; one of the smallest and least important at the time was the monastery of Kells. As a result of his mission to the Picts, however, Columba's most important monastery, and what was to become the dominant monastic centre in the British Isles, was established in the year 565 on a remote island off the west coast of Scotland. This island of Iona, granted to Columba by the Pictish king, became the mother house of the Columban monasteries in Ireland and of an increasing number of Columban monasteries in Scotland and England during the next hundred years. Above all, it was the monastery of Iona that was to bring to Northumbria elements of Irish scholarship, expertise and art. But all this was still in the future when St Columba (known also as Columcille) died in 597, the year in which St Augustine first arrived in Kent to convert the pagan Anglo-Saxons.

It was in these closing years of the 6th century that the mission led by the monk Columbanus from the Irish monastery of Bangor took the learning and traditions of the Irish Church much further afield, to found the monastery of Luxeuil, in Burgundy, to leave St Gallus among the pagan Alemanni of Switzerland and, finally, to found in Lombardy the monastery of Bobbio. St Columbanus was only the first of a long line of Irish monks who were to travel to the continent during the next three centuries.

Meanwhile, in Kent, St Augustine and his successor at Canterbury had strengthened the position of the Church, established there from Rome, and by 625 the conversion of the northern kingdom of Northumbria was being successfully undertaken by Bishop Paulinus. But, immediately, the Northumbrians suffered a fierce defeat by their bitter enemies, the Britons of Wales, and in the turmoil of the aftermath the Northumbrians again returned to paganism. It was nearly a decade before peace returned. Then, in 635, the Northumbrian King Oswald, having himself become a Christian while in exile in Ireland, turned not to Rome but to the Irish Church for assistance in restoring the Christian faith in his country. When the monk-bishop, Aidan, from the monastery of Iona was sent with a group of monks, King Oswald provided the island of Lindisfarne as the site to found their church.

Soon not only Lindisfarne but also the whole of Northumbria had Columban monasteries, closely linked with Iona and influenced by the Irish Church both ecclesiastically and culturally. Bishop Aidan was succeeded at Lindisfarne by bishops sent by Iona who maintained Irish observances. Before long, a bitter controversy arose over the practices of the Irish Church. The new Roman Church at Canterbury protested that the Irish outdated method of calculating Easter, as well as the Irish form of tonsure and other matters of ecclesiastical discipline, were contrary to the custom of the universal Church. This dispute led to the calling of the Council of Whitby (in the year 664), at which the spokesmen for the Irish practices eventually appeared to agree that the Roman practices were better. But in spite of this apparent agreement, some of the Columban monks and bishops in England remained dissatisfied. Bishop Colman, in particular, left Lindisfarne with many Irish and English followers for Ireland, where in the northern monasteries the Celtic customs continued for another forty years. The mother house, Iona, persisted in the Irish calculation of Easter for even longer, and it was the year 715 before the Iona monks were persuaded to change.

Although the Roman practices were accepted from the year 664, in Northumbria, especially at Lindisfarne, Irish influences survived in several ways. Its abbots and bishops continued for another twenty years to be men associated with Ireland or with Aidan, the first bishop of Columban Lindisfarne. A much more lasting link with Irish scholarship and culture continued in the Irish monasteries themselves, for many English monks and scholars travelled to Ireland to be educated in the schools and to study under Irish teachers. There they were both instructed and also, according to Bede, provided with many books to read.

Aldhelm of Malmesbury complained in bitter terms of the large number of

Ezra the scribe from the Codex Amiatinus. Biblioteca Laurenziana, Florence

scholars who flocked to Ireland when they could have received their education and learning from the Roman school at Canterbury. Aldhelm's anxiety arose from the interest of Irish scholarship in secular and pagan texts along with Christian ones.

The Irish schools were famous for their teaching of the Latin language and for their scholarly study of the Latin classics as well as of the sacred texts and commentaries. But although there is widespread evidence at Iona, in England and on the continent of the fame of the Irish monastery schools and of the scholarly learning of Irish monks, little of it has survived in Ireland itself from the 7th and 8th centuries. There are no records of the teachers and the schools, few survivors of the books of the Irish monastery libraries and scriptoria and no copies of the texts of the classical authors they held so dear. From the beginning of their missions abroad, however, the Irish monks had taken their scholarship and their books with them and these can be traced, both directly and indirectly, in the Irish continental monasteries during later centuries.

Irish monks felt none of the reluctance of St Jerome or the scorn of Pope Gregory the Great towards the study of pagan classical literature. Despite their reputation for teaching pure and correct Latin, their own writing in England and on the continent is often ornate and fantastic with a delight in obscure words, both Latin and Greek.

Northumbrian scholarship was heir not only to Irish and Columban traditions, however, but to those of Anglo-Saxon origin from Canterbury. Archbishop Theodore and Hadrian, abbot of the monastery at Canterbury, had brought fresh traditions when they founded in the year 671 a school at Canterbury modelled upon the education and scholarship of Rome.

Hadrian came from Byzantine Italy, and the students who were rapidly attracted to his Canterbury school were introduced to the learning and art of not only Italy but the East as well. Of even greater significance to the Northumbrians was the stimulus to Italian scholarship and art brought to them directly by Benedict Biscop, founder of the monastery of St Peter at Wearmouth, in 674, and of the sister monastery of St Paul seven miles away at Jarrow, in 681. These were centres of strict Benedictine monasticism but with an emphasis on intellectual pursuits. From his frequent journeys to Rome, Benedict Biscop brought back the ideas of Italy along with books to build up large libraries, plus glasswork and painted panels for the monastery buildings at Wearmouth and Jarrow. By the beginning of the 8th century they formed one of the most flourishing centres of scholarship in Western Europe.

It was into Benedict Biscop's care that the boy Bede was put in the year 680 at Wearmouth. He moved to Jarrow when the sister house was founded and for more than fifty years devoted himself there to the outstanding scholarship which was to make his name known everywhere, 'a new sun in the west, ordained to illuminate the whole globe', as Notker Balbulus of St Gall described him (Dorothy Whitelock. *After Bede*).

The magnificent library and scriptorium at Jarrow provided the essential basis for Bede's scholarly activity. Among the many books that came from the scriptorium were three copies of the text of the Bible that provides the closest link with the Vulgate of St

Jerome's day. One of these has survived complete, the Codex Amiatinus in the Laurentian Library in Florence. It is to this codex that the text of the Lindisfarne Gospels is related.

In 735, the year in which Bede died, the archbishopric of York was established and there Archbishop Egbert, who had studied under Bede, founded a further Anglo-Saxon school that was to become famous for scholarship. York, too, had a large library, strong in patristic and Christian works though weak in classical texts. It was there that Alcuin established the reputation that was to take him to Charlemagne's court to lead the revival of education and learning throughout Europe.

These disparate traditions in 7th- and 8th-century Northumbria are the background to that mingling of scholarship, expertise and art which was to produce in the Northumbrian scriptoria those splendid Insular manuscripts that show affinities with the Book of Kells.

The time of this activity was short, and most of the books of the libraries and scriptoria have vanished. Scandinavian raids on Lindisfarne began in 793 and Jarrow was plundered in the following year. By 835, Lindisfarne, Wearmouth/Jarrow and York were reduced to pale shadows of their former greatness. The destruction wrought by the Scandinavian raiders was no less in the Irish monasteries. Their raids on the island of Iona led the monks to move the mother house of the Columban monasteries to Kells in the year 806. The small monastery at Kells thereby became one of Ireland's major monastic centres, but there are no records to tell us of its monks or their activities.

Captions to the plates are on page 4

11

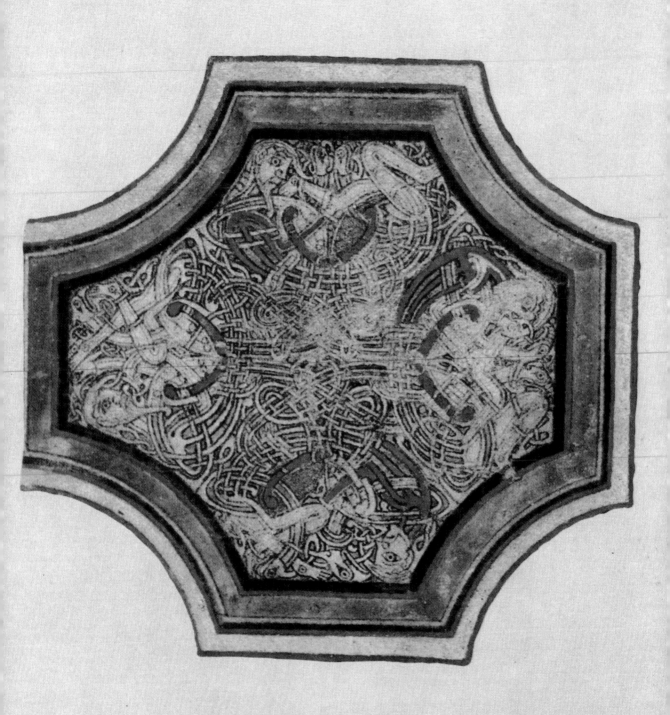

bȝenerαȝιo

Eata pauperes spu quoniam
ipsorum est regnum caelorum·
Eata mices quoniam ipsi possi
❀ ❀ ❀ debunt terram ⸻ ⸸ ⸱⸸
Eata qui lugent nunc quoniam·
❀ ❀ ❀ ipsi consulabuntur ⸻ ⸱⸸
Eata quiessuriunt & sitiunt
iusticiam quoniam ipsi satu
❀ ❀ ❀ ❀ rabuntur ⸻ ⸸ ⸱⸸ ⸸ ⸱⸸
Eata misericordes quoniam·
ipsi misericordiam consequntr
Eata mundo corde· quoniam
ipsi dm uidebu⸻nt ⸸ ⸱⸸ ⸱⸸
Eata pacifici quoniam filii di
❀ ❀ ❀ uocabuntur ⸻ ⸸ ⸱ ⸸ ⸸
Eata qui persecutionem pati
untur. propter. iusticiam quoni

Ue autem praegnatibus &

nutriantibus inillis diebus

Orate autem utnonfiat fuga

uestra hieme uel sabbato

Erit enim tunc tribulatio magna

qualis nonfuit abinitio mun

di usque modo neque fi

Et nisi breuiata fuissent dies

illi nonfiera salua om

nis caro sedpropter electos bre

uiabuntur dies illi

Tunc siquis uobis dixerit ecce

hicxps autillic nolite credere

Surgent enim seudoxpi &

seudo profetae & dabunt

signamagna & prodigia itainerro

rem inducantur si fieri potest etiam

22

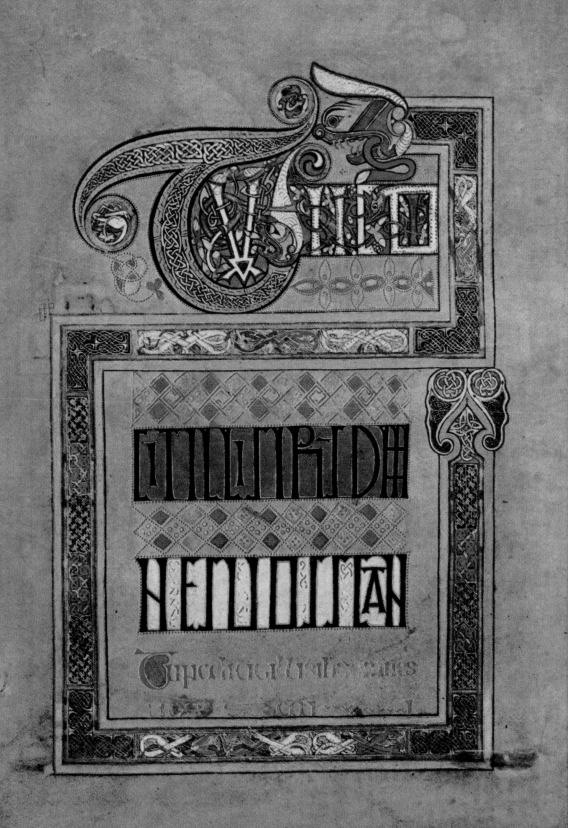

ETBERE ...

sabbati quaeluicescit
Inprima. sabbata uenit maria
magdalene. & altera maria uide-
re·sepulchrum & ecce terrae mo-
tus factus est magnus angelus
enim dñi decaelo dhscenoit. & ac
cedens Reuoluit lapidem & sedebat supereum · Erat autem as
pectus eius sicut fulgor & uesti
mentum eius candidum sicut nix·
Praetimore· autem eius exterriti
sunt custodes · & factusuic uel
motui

Responcdens autem car chrisdixta

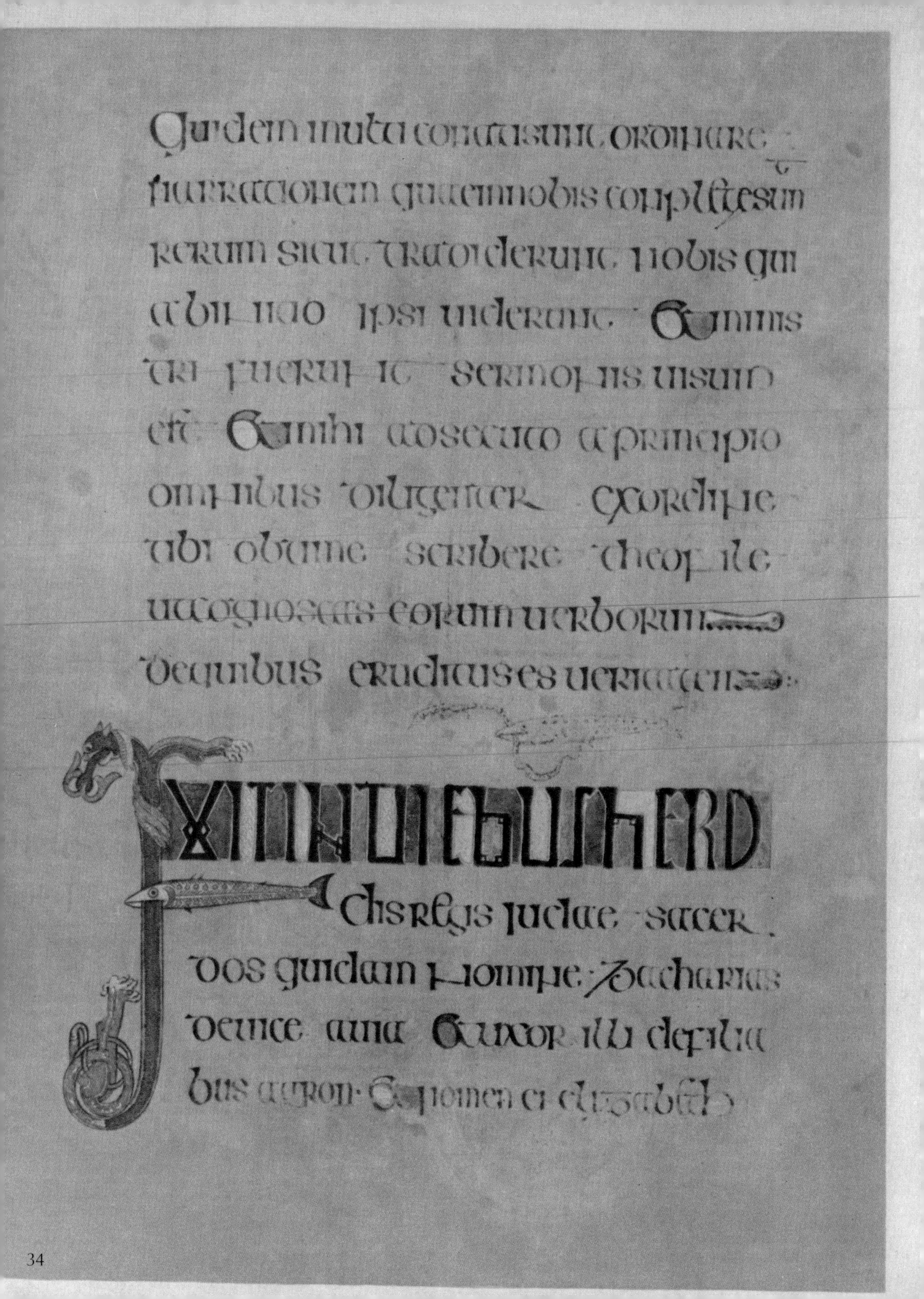

Quidem multa conatisunt ordinare
narrationem quaeinnobis conpletęsum
rerum sicut tradiderunt nobis qui
abinitio ipsi uiderunt Etunius
eri fuerunt sermonis uisum
et Etmihi adsecuto aprincipio
omnibus diligenter exordine
ubi obtime scribere theophile
uccognoscas eorum uerborum
dequibus eruditus es ueritatem

FUITINDIEBUSHERD
chis regis iudee sacer
dos quidam nomine zacharias
deuice anna Etuxor illi defilia
bus aaron Etnomen ei elizabeth

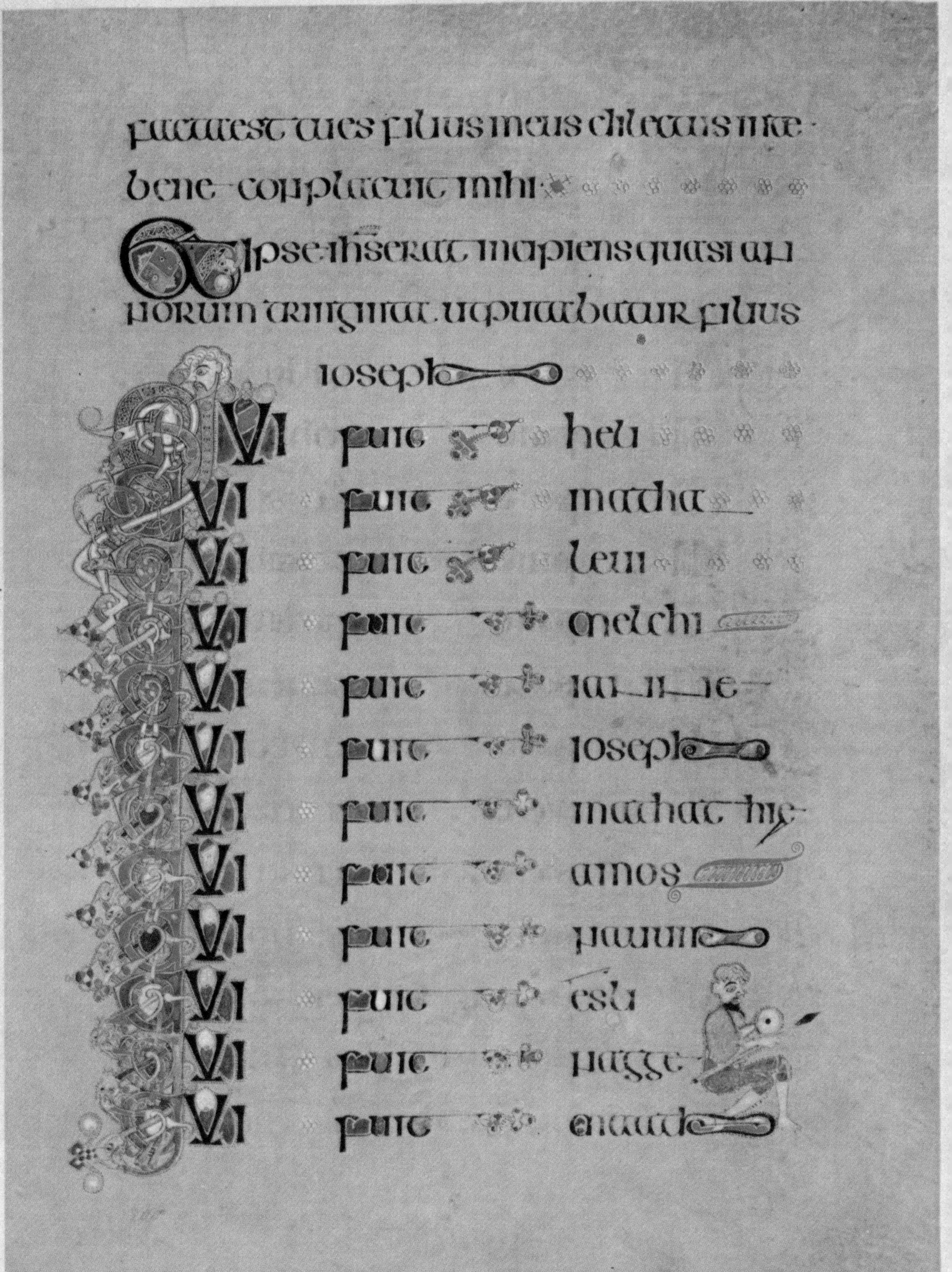

piacuit est tu es filius meus dilectus inte

bene · conplacuit mihi ·

Et ipse ihserut incipiens quasi an

norum triginta · ut putabatur filius

ioseph

VI fuit heli

VI fuit matha

VI fuit leui

VI fuit melchi

VI fuit iaruhie

VI fuit ioseph

VI fuit mathat hic

VI fuit amos

VI fuit nauum

VI fuit esli

VI fuit nagge

VI fuit emath

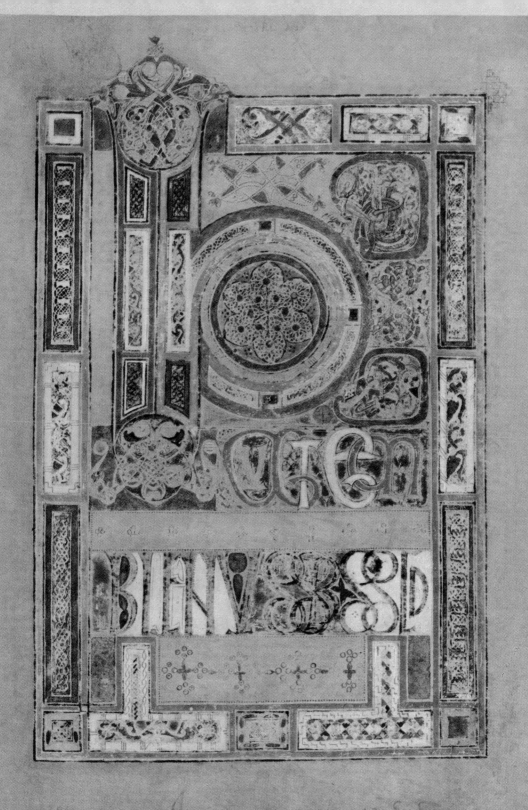

40

43

Omne · quod dat mihi pater ad me ·

ueniet — & eum qui uenit ad me non eiciam

foras :· Quia descendi de caelo non ut faciam

seduoluntatem eius qui me misit :·

Haec est autem uoluntas eius qui m

sit me pater is ut omne · quod dedit

mihi non perdam ex eo sedresuscitem

illum innouissimo die · Haec est enim

uoluntas patris mei qui misit me · ut om

nis qui uidit filium & credit in eum ha

beat uitam aeternam & resuscitabo

eum innouissimo die ·

Murmurabant ergo iudaei deillo

quia dixisset — & dosumpanis qui de

caelo discendi & dicebant nonne hic

es his filius ioseph cuius nos nouimus

patrem & matrem quomodo ergo dicit

INTERROGABAT ev

XPS FILIUS DI

NOS AUTEM O

DEBTAS FILI

TEM MOETERIS UIR

GE ARTN

MENO IUINA

TERROGARE

RESPONDENS

INTEMPLO QU

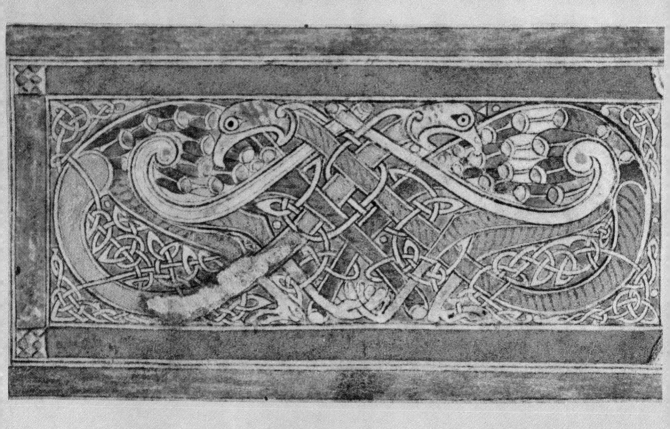

47

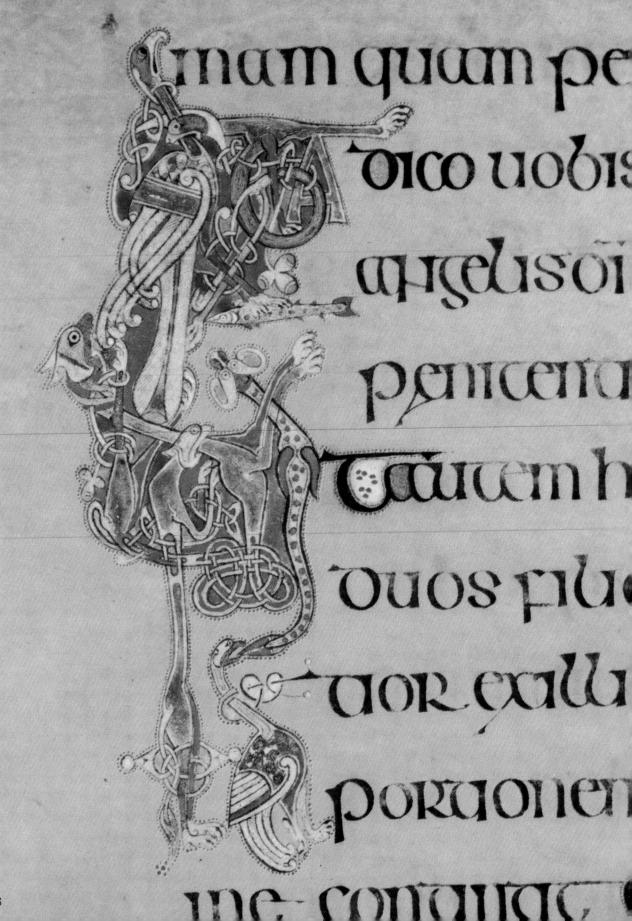

inam quam pe

dico uobis

angelus dī

penitent

tantem h

duos filio

uor exulta

porttonem

me contugat

III The scribes and their texts

EVERY MONASTERY needed its own stock of working copies of Bibles, psalters, missals and other texts for the ecclesiastical life of the community. It also needed documents for the running of the monastery, ranging from a copy of the Rule that the monastery followed and its Penitential to business documents such as deeds and letters. Books for religious study and for moral instruction were also needed, plus commentaries on the biblical texts, the writings of the Church Fathers and some lives of saints. The monastery school also needed its texts, and a monastery where scholarly studies were pursued required a much wider range of books in its library. Every copy of every book had to be made in a monastery scriptorium. Although there were monks everywhere who could write sufficiently well to make copies of documents, not every monastery could undertake the production of copies of books, an activity that required specialist skills and crafts. Far fewer were the monasteries in which there were the expertise and artistry to undertake the production of highly decorated books.

Books were borrowed by one monastery from another in order to make copies. The scriptorium that was able to produce books did so both for its own monastery and also to meet the requests of other monasteries.

The work of the scribes in producing legible and correct copies required abilities gained from a thorough education in a monastery school: a sound knowledge of Latin grammar, vocabulary and syntax, training in writing and extensive experience in reading and interpreting the writing of other scribes. Many books that issued from scriptoria show very serious failings in some or even all of these abilities, for even the best-trained scribe was faced with daunting problems if the exemplar that he was copying had come from the hands of an ill-educated, insufficiently trained or careless scribe. Faced with writing in which the text could be only partially recognized, with frequent errors and omissions and with many words unintelligibly abbreviated, the copyist could not hope to produce a good text. If his own Latin were poor, he was likely to reproduce everything seen in his exemplar, including its errors and inevitably adding some of his own. If his Latin were good he would try to correct what he recognized as errors in the exemplar, but in doing so he was likely to corrupt the text through misunderstanding. What a scribe wrote was often corrected by a monk with better Latin or more experience, but some errors would remain unnoticed or would at times be miscorrected.

All these features of copying are to be seen in the Book of Kells. Its text is full of errors of many kinds, very few of which have been corrected – errors of spelling, errors

73

in Latin grammar and even errors showing inability to understand the meaning of the Latin.

Although there are features in its decoration that place the Book of Kells apart from other books that have survived from the 7th, 8th and perhaps early 9th centuries, it cannot be considered entirely by itself as an isolated phenomenon. Not only is it a part of the European tradition, but it shows, in particular, a significant relationship to the group of manuscripts produced mainly in Northumbria and Ireland (also on the continent), many being copies of the Gospels and all arising from the Insular traditions and expertise.

Within this group of manuscripts there has always been great difficulty in distinguishing between Irish manuscripts and Anglo-Saxon manuscripts. The background from which this uncertainty arises has been described earlier, in the picture given of the two traditions in Northumbria: the Irish presence and influences of the original Columban monasteries, and the Anglo-Saxon and Roman influences of the Benedictine monasteries. Irish-trained scribes were almost certainly to be found in Northumbria as well as in Ireland; Anglo-Saxon influences could easily have been transported from Northumbria to Ireland. This mixture of traditions was also transferred to some of the continental monasteries by Irish and Anglo-Saxon missionaries. The manuscripts of the group can all be identified by their Insular features, even though some features of the script are described as Anglo-Saxon and others as Irish. For some of them, the monastery scriptorium from which they came and even the names of the scribes are known, but for others, the problems of identifying the location and date of their origin remain. To trace the relationships between these Insular manuscripts is a matter of great technical detail, but some points of comparison can be made fairly simply between the Book of Kells and a few of the Latin manuscripts of the group. The ones that concern us, with possible location and date of origin, are:

The Book of Durrow, Ireland or Northumbria, second half of the 7th century

The Lindisfarne Gospels, Lindisfarne, end of the 7th century

The Echternach Gospels, Northumbria or the continent, beginning of the 8th century

The Durham Gospels, Ireland or Northumbria, beginning of the 8th century

The Lichfield Gospels, a Welsh centre, second half of the 8th century

The Book of Armagh, Armagh, 807

Four aspects of the text of the Book of Kells need to be examined in a comparison between it and these other manuscripts: the total original contents of the book, the wording of the text, the style of the writing and the style of the decoration. Each of these aspects has to be considered separately, for each provides its own basis for drawing conclusions, and at times the evidence is conflicting.

74

The text of the Book of Kells contains not just the four Gospels, but also the traditional accompaniments: the Canon Tables, *Breves causae, Argumenta* and glosses (although the glosses are incomplete). There may have been other customary contents, too, in the missing folios at the beginning and end of the book.

The Canon Tables, references for comparison among numbered sections (approximately equivalent to the modern verses; the text of the Gospels was not divided into the now familiar chapters and verses), established by Eusebius of Caesarea in the 4th century, were regularly placed at the beginning to make comparison among all four Gospels possible. The *Breves causae* for each Gospel had their origin in an old tradition of providing a summary referring to numbered divisions of the text (approximately equivalent to the modern chapter), and each Gospel normally had this summary immediately before its text. Each Gospel is normally also accompanied by the *Argumentum*, a collection of anecdotal details about each of the four Evangelists, and the glosses, lists of the Hebrew names appearing in it.

There is no regular order of appearance for these accompaniments, but some part of them is usually placed before each Gospel, except in the case of Kells and Durrow, where the texts of the Gospels proceed uninterrupted from Matthew to John, while the accompaniments, in an exceptionally complicated sequence, are placed quite separately. Kells has them all as Preliminaries to the book and Durrow has them mainly as Preliminaries, with two of the *Breves* appearing after the Gospel text of John. Moreover, although there was no traditional established text for the *Breves causae* and the *Argumenta*, it is remarkable that the Kells text for these is virtually identical to the Durrow text, which in turn has textual similarities to the prefaces of the Echternach Gospels.

It, therefore, seems certain that in both planning and execution the texts of these Preliminaries in Kells were directly copied from Durrow (or from a copy that had a text practically identical with that of Durrow). And yet, most of the Preliminaries in Kells are virtually unusable. The Canon Tables are magnificently presented (Pls 1, 2 and 3), but, as the relevant sections in the text have not been marked with their section numbers, the numbers in the Canon Tables serve no practical purpose. Similarly, the splendid appearance of the *Breves causae* (Pls 5, 6 and 7) diverts attention from the fact that they, too, are of little use, as few of the numbers needed in these summaries and none in the text of the Gospels themselves have been written in. It is clear that Kells was not intended to be used for scholarly study. Not that the summaries were of very great use in Durrow either, for they were compiled from the Old Latin text and do not easily correspond with either the 'mixed' text of Kells or the Vulgate text of Durrow.

The revisions carried out by St Jerome in his translation had been widely accepted and in the Roman Church had generally replaced the Old Latin text. But the Celtic Church had been more conservative, retaining many words and phrases of the Old Latin text in its version of the Vulgate. It is this mixed text that is generally associated with the Irish Church and is found in the Book of Kells and the Book of Armagh, the

Lichfield Gospels and a number of other Gospels. The Book of Durrow has a fairly normal form of the Vulgate text, while the Lindisfarne Gospels has the particularly Italian form of the Vulgate found in the Codex Amiatinus.

Even where there are close relationships among types of texts from a number of manuscripts, there are, of course, many discrepancies between the text of one manuscript and another. On the other hand, dissimilar texts may show identical errors, indicating a relationship that is not easy to explain. Such a relationship exists between the text of the Book of Kells and that of the Book of Durrow, for several nonsensical blunders in the Latin appear in both manuscripts. The virtual identity of the texts of the Preliminaries in the two manuscripts has already been described, and this common text includes some blunders. But the appearance of common blunders in the texts of the Gospels is more difficult to explain. There are several indications, however, that the text of Kells came from more than one manuscript, since phrases and words from different sources have been jumbled together, thereby making nonsense of the Latin. Whether the text of the Book of Kells was compiled by scribes who consulted and copied from various differing texts, or whether it was copied from a single exemplar that already contained text from various differing sources cannot be ascertained. In either case some text came from the Book of Durrow or from a manuscript copied from it or by it.

The layout of the pages of the text consists of long lines written across the page (Pl. 44) although a more designed layout is provided for situations in which there is repetition, as in the Beatitudes (Pl. 20) and the Genealogy (Pl. 35). Strangely, the first four pages of the first Gospel are written in double columns. The truly striking aspects of the text, however, lie in the actual writing and in the textual decoration. The two are inextricably intertwined in a way that is not even attempted in any other surviving Insular manuscript, whether Irish or Northumbrian.

The letters are written in the half-uncial style found in a number of the Insular manuscripts. The custom of using solely capital letters had passed, even in their rounded form of uncial script. The half-uncials still retain some capital forms (the enlarged detail of *f.* 179v, Pl. 46, first word *interrogabet*) but they are the same size as the other letters. The script of the Book of Kells shows at times the connection of letters to one another (enlarged detail of *f.* 170v, Pl. 46, third line *terrogare*), which characterizes the development of cursive minuscule. A few pages of the Kells script have compressed forms at the ends of lines or in the last line of the page (Pl. 8), which suggest minuscule.

The shapes of the letters are remarkably strong, written with expertise and confidence in symmetrical lines. Vertical strokes, both straight and rounded, are penned thickly with bold triangular pennant heads. Horizontal strokes are thin and are frequently used to join letters, sometimes with a slight triangular terminal. The detail of the strokes can easily be followed in the enlargements of Pls 46 and 48.

At times horizontal strokes are exaggeratedly extended, both in the middle of words (especially the almost horizontal stroke of N) and at the end of sentences and lines, to fill up the space or to connect with some decoration. The last letter of a line is frequently distorted into an elongated shape (Pl. 20, fourth line reads: *debunt terram*).

The abbreviation of words by the scribes of the Book of Kells is restrained and is restricted almost entirely to contractions: IHS = *Jesus*, XPS = *Christus*, DNS = *Dominus*, DI = *Dei*, sps = *Spiritus* and scs = *Sanctus*, h = *autem*, n = *non*, st = *sunt*. The presence of an abbreviated word is usually shown by a mark above the contraction (*f.* 179v, Pl. 46, line 2 is abbreviated *christus filius dei*, while line 3 begins with the decorated IHS for *Jesus*, with a fish to mark the contraction).

The practice found in many manuscripts of run-overs, carrying a line of text over into a gap in the line above or below is called by Irish scribes 'turn in the path' (*cor fa casam*) or 'head under the wing' (*ceann fa eitil*). In the Book of Kells such run-overs occur very frequently and confusingly, with ends of lines completed in the line above or below and marked not just by the usual slanting lines, but with a small figure or animal pointing out the direction in which to read (*f.* 19v, Pl. 7, the last two lines of the plate have to be read: *filium Iesum. Natiuitatem Jesu adnuntiat angelus pas – toribus. Et acci*). Similarly, on Pl. 44, the fourth line turns back to the third: *Quia discendi de caelo non ut faciam – voluntatem meam – sed voluntatem eius qui me misit* (John VI: 38).

Of the scribes themselves we know nothing beyond what their writing tells us. The last folio of the book may have included a colophon on the final page to provide some information about its production, but the last folios are missing. Nor is there any mention of the production of the Book of Kells in any records, annals or lives of saints.

In *Codices Latini Antiquiores*, Dr E. A. Lowe recognized in the Book of Kells the work of several scribes. Françoise Henry in her text accompanying the reproductions, published in 1974, distinguishes at least three different hands, represented in the Kells reproductions in this volume by:

Hand A   Pls 6, 7 and 44
Hand B   Pls 8, 26 and perhaps 34
Hand C   Pls 20, 21 and 35

Although she recognizes the close similarities among these hands, she finds different approaches; she suggests that they are the work of at least three scribes: A writes in a slightly archaic and restrained way with a massive and compact script; B shows more exuberance with coloured inks in the Preliminaries and is inclined to compressed writing at the foot of pages, with flourishes in a way that is reminiscent of minuscule; C is responsible for writing the greatest part of the book with a freer script than A and with slightly higher letters.

The selection of pages for reproduction here highlights the magnificent illustrated pages and, thereby, gives an incomplete impression of the Book of Kells as a whole, for the greater part of the book consists of over six hundred pages of text. When one looks through all these text pages there is certainly a general impression of the work of a

The beginning of Mark from the Book of Durrow (*f*. 86R). Trinity College Library, Dublin

number of different hands, but apart from the differences of detail described by Mlle Henry it does not seem possible to identify further ways in which the majuscule letters have been formed by different scribes.

So, unless we have the work of one scribe who writes in several different styles, the Book of Kells was written by a number of scribes, splendidly trained in the pen strokes required for the formation of these imposing letters. The strokes made in the formation of the letters can be identified clearly in the enlarged details (*f*. 179v, Pl. 46, Pl. 48). It is tempting to assume that these scribes must have been trained in the same school, but there are close resemblances in the scripts of a number of other manuscripts. The majuscule letters in the Lichfield Gospels are remarkably similar. The Insular majuscule of the Book of Durrow (*f*. 86R) or of the Lindisfarne Gospels, however, is very different.

The part played by the scribes in the decoration of the text pages is uncertain, although it is clear from the writing of the text and some of its decoration that careful

78

tes ihm duxerunt adcaifan principem

sacerdotum ubi scribae & seniores·

conuenerunt· petrus autem sequeba

tur eum alonge usque inatrium prin

cipes sacerdotum & ingressus inatrio

sedebat cum ministris ut uideret fine

ra· Principes autem sacerdotum &

omne concilium querebant falsum

testimonium contra ihm uteum morti

traderent & non inuenerunt cum & cum

multi falsi testes accesserent· Nouissi

me autem uenerunt duo falsi testes &

dixerunt hic dixit possum distruere

templum di & post triduum aedifica

re illud surgens princeps sacerdotu

aitilli nihil respondes adea quae is

testificantur aduersumte ihs autem

tacebat & princeps sacerdotum ait

illi adiurote perdm uiuum ut dicas

nobis situes xps filius di dictilli ihs

Page of text from the Lichfield Gospels. Lichfield Cathedral

planning was required of the scribe while he was carrying out his task of copying. Whether the scribe also acted as decorator of the text, or whether he merely indicated the letters to be represented subsequently by the painter, cannot be determined; too little is known of the precise activities of both writing and painting. It is possible that the scribe, having finished his page of text, put down his pen and took up his brush and painted, but this assumes that in addition to his high level of expertise in calligraphy he also had very considerable artistic ability.

The amount of planning needed during the writing of the text, for the decoration of capital letters and words at the beginning of lines, was considerable. Although the Eusebian sections are not numbered in the text of the Book of Kells the beginning of most of the sections is marked by a decorated capital or word, and this decoration was allowed for during the writing of the text by leaving sufficient space, not only at the beginning of that line but frequently in the following lines of script (Pl. 21 and especially the enlarged detail of Pl. 48, but less happily in Pl. 8). Some whole pages had to be planned in advance to achieve a particular artistic effect for the whole of the text on a page, as in the Beatitudes where the letter *b* for the repetition of *beata* is planned as a decoration stretching down the entire page (Pl. 20) and, similarly, in the Genealogy where the repetition of the word *qui* is used to produce an intricate and intertwined decoration (Pl. 35). The larger decorated phrases in the middle of the text were similarly allowed for by the scribe (Pls 6 and 34).

The relationship of the Book of Kells to other manuscripts reveals many problems that cannot be limited just to those connections that can be identified from the text and the script, for the Book of Kells is a product of the artist as well as of the scribe. But for the moment let us bring together those links that have been identified so far.

There is undoubtedly some fairly close connection between the text of the Book of Kells and that of the Book of Durrow. Both the planning of the contents and the execution of the text show some striking similarities that go far beyond coincidence. The closely similar Kells/Durrow text of the Preliminaries has also some similarities with the text found in the Echternach Gospels. The elements of connection between Kells and Durrow in the Gospels text are more difficult to account for in view of the 'mixed' nature of the Kells text compared with the fairly typical Vulgate text of Durrow, and suggest that the Kells Gospels are based on more than one manuscript text. There seems to be no other surviving manuscript with a Gospels text that provides a recognizable link with Kells, even where we might look for similarities in other manuscripts with the mixed text favoured by Irish communties: the Durham Gospels or the Book of Armagh. The very special Vulgate text of the Lindisfarne Gospels (one of the few manuscripts about whose origin there can be no doubt) certainly shares no links with either Kells or Durrow. In the knowledge that only very little has survived from the libraries and the output of the scriptoria of both Northumbrian and Irish monasteries, we must recognize that the text provides insufficient evidence for any firm conclusions.

The nature of the script also provides uncertain evidence. Within the range of scripts that can be grouped together under the name Insular majuscule, there are elements that are identified as being of Irish origin. The nature of some Northumbrian monasteries with strongly Irish communities suggests, however, that Irish traditions and influences could have been expected there, as well as in the monasteries of Ireland and the Columban monastic centre at Iona. The links could have worked the other way, however, with Northumbrian influences reaching Irish monasteries. The closest parallel to the script of the Book of Kells is that of the Lichfield Gospels, and this suggests that the expertise in writing this remarkable script was transportable and could be found in monasteries outside Ireland or Northumbria. The style of script in the Lindisfarne Gospels, on the other hand, has close similarities with that of the Echternach Gospels and the Durham Gospels and there are some similarities with the script of the Book of Durrow.

Both the date and place of origin of the Book of Kells remain uncertain. The question of the date is an important factor in view of the effects on the monasteries of the Scandinavian raiders, but there is still disagreement on whether the Book of Kells is a product of the second half of the 8th century or of the early 9th century. The suggestions for the location of the scriptorium that produced the Book of Kells range widely: an Irish monastery (perhaps Kells), the Columban monastery at Iona, a Northumbrian monastery (perhaps Lindisfarne) or, on the evidence of the style of letters on inscrip‚ tions, even a Columban monastery in Pictland. A scriptorium able to undertake such a masterpiece as the Book of Kells must have had quite extraordinary resources of both calligraphic and artistic expertise. It seems unlikely that the small monastery at Kells could provide this before the Columban centre moved from Iona to Kells in the year 806. There was certainly a scriptorium at Iona while the Columban centre was there. It has been suggested, therefore, that the work of the Book of Kells was undertaken by the community in Iona and that the Book of Kells (perhaps still uncompleted) was brought by the Columban monks to Kells. The scriptoria about which we know most (even that is little enough) and which were on a scale to produce major manuscripts are those of Lindisfarne and Wearmouth/Jarrow, but it has to be recognized that not all the aspects of the text, the script and the illustration in the Book of Kells conform easily with the tradition and output of these Northumbrian monasteries. Of the 8th‚century Irish monasteries, their libraries and their scriptoria almost nothing has survived.

The beginning of Matthew from the Lindisfarne Gospels (*f.* 27R). British Library

IV The illumination and the artists

'THIS BOOK contains the harmony of the four Evangelists according to Jerome, where for almost every page there are different designs, distinguished by varied colours. Here you may see the face of majesty, divinely drawn, here the mystic symbols of the Evangelists, each with wings, now six, now four, now two; here the Eagle, there the Calf, here the Man and there the Lion, and other forms almost infinite. Look at them superficially with the ordinary casual glance, and you would think it an erasure, and not tracery. Fine craftsmanship is all about you, but you might not notice it. Look more keenly at it, and you will penetrate to the very shrine of art. You will make out intricacies, so delicate and subtle, so exact and compact, so full of knots and links, with colours so fresh and vivid, that you might say that all this was the work of an angel, and not of a man. For my part the oftener I see the book, and the more carefully I study it, the more I am lost in ever fresh amazement, and I see more and more wonders in the book.'

So wrote Giraldus Cambrensis in his *Topographia Hiberniae*, an account of his travels in Ireland in 1185 and following years. He was describing a wonderful book, the most marvellous thing of all the marvels of Kildare. No such book associated with Kildare has survived and there are those who believe that Giraldus was really describing the Book of Kells. Although that is merely speculation, the splendid description does tell us exactly how we should look at the artistry of the Book of Kells. It is not something that can be appreciated at a rapid glance. As Giraldus makes clear, the more you study the details of the ornament, in the text pages as well as in the full-page decorations, the more you see of the imagination of the artists and the intricacy of their art.

It is possible in a range of other manuscripts, particularly the Insular manuscripts, to find parallels to Kells for individual features, but nowhere else do all these features appear together and in such profusion. The uniqueness of the Book of Kells lies in this variety of decoration and ornamentation produced with such complexity and in such quantity.

It is difficult to know exactly how the overall arrangement of the illustration for the Book of Kells was planned, particularly as there are perhaps thirty folios missing, with the probability that these include some fully decorated pages. If we look first at the Gospels themselves, it seems that the plan was to have at the beginning of each Gospel three fully illustrated pages: the symbols of the four Evangelists; a portrait of the Evangelist whose Gospel follows; and a highly decorated page for the opening words

83

of the Gospel. This is exactly what appears at the beginning of Matthew (Pls 10, 11 and 13) and John (Pls 40, 41, 42, and 43); but the other two Gospels lack part of this arrangement, with no portrait of Mark before his Gospel and neither the symbols of the four Evangelists nor a portrait before Luke's Gospel.

In general, such a plan conforms with what is found in some other copies of the Gospels. In the Lindisfarne Gospels each Gospel is preceded by a 'carpet' page of overall design, a portrait of the Evangelist (Lindisfarne f. 209v) and also a partially decorated page for the opening words (Lindisfarne f. 29R). The Book of Durrow plan before each Gospel seems to consist of the symbol of the Evangelist, a carpet page and a partially decorated page for the opening words.

St Matthew's Gospel is frequently treated as having two beginnings, with what is called the Book of the Generation (Pl. 13 and Lindisfarne f. 27R) regarded as a separate section, and a second beginning made at the birth of Christ. The illustrated pages in Kells show this second beginning with the portrait of Christ, a full-page decoration and the highly decorated Chi-Rho page for the beginning of our verse 18, where the account of the birth of Christ begins (Pls 14–19). The Lindisfarne Gospels also show the second beginning (Lindisfarne f. 29R).

There are also large illustrated pages within the text of the Gospels, at the highly significant points in the story. The Arrest of Christ, with an illustrated page and highly decorated text (Pls 22 and 23); the Crucifixion (Pl. 25), faced by a blank page which may have been intended for a full-page painting; in Mark, the Crucifixion (Pl. 30); in Luke, the Temptation (Pls 36 and 37) and the Resurrection (Pl. 38). There are no such illustrated pages in John. We can only try to deduce from the material that has survived what the original plan was, what was planned and not executed, what was executed but subsequently lost.

Throughout the whole of the Book of Kells one of the most striking features is the repeated emphasis on the four Evangelists through their symbols, the Man for Matthew, the Lion for Mark, the Calf for Luke and the Eagle for John, depicted again and again together but each time with a variation in presentation: in the tympanum above the Canon Tables (Pls 1, 2 and 3), in the elaborately framed full-page illustrations before the Gospels (Pls 10, 27 and 40).

In the first chapter of the prophet Ezekiel, a vision of four, winged, human figures is described, each with four faces, those of a man, a lion, an ox and an eagle. The Apocalypse (IV, 2ff.) includes a similar vision of four figures, a lion, an ox, a man and an eagle, each with six wings. The allocation of symbol to Evangelist at first varied, as did the order of the Gospels, but the Book of Kells shows both as they had been established since St Jerome. It also depicts each of the symbols mainly in fairly natural form with appropriate heads, hands, claws or hooves (although there are exceptions as in Pl. 2, where the third figure has a calf's head on an eagle's body). In some manuscripts they appear as human forms with animal heads, in others as animals with hands (there are two instances of this in Kells) and human feet.

84

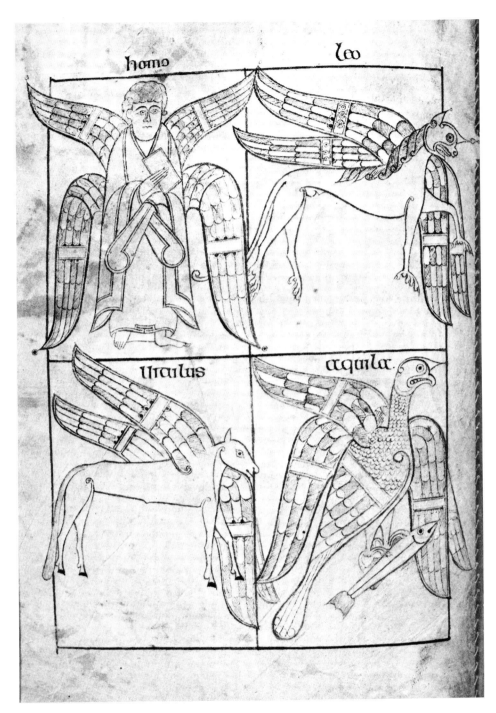

The four symbols of the Evangelists from the Book of Armagh (*f.* 32v). Trinity College Library, Dublin

The four-symbol presentation in one page is found in several other Insular Gospels–the Book of Durrow, the Lichfield Gospels, the Book of Armagh (Armagh *f.* 32v)–but occurs only once in each book and not repeatedly as in Kells. The undecorated and uncoloured stark presentation in Armagh makes a striking contrast with the richness in Kells.

The ten pages of decorated Canon Tables in the Book of Kells are remarkable for their sumptuous presentation in an architectural structure of arches and arcades, columns and discs (Pls 1, 2 and 3). In those Insular manuscripts that have Canon Tables there is nothing similar, although the use of architectural columns is found in the Lindisfarne Gospels, but in a very restrained style.

The great fully illustrated pages are of several kinds: the portraits, the Evangelists' symbols, the introductory text pages to each of the Gospels, the decorated text and illustration to the story, and a 'carpet' page.

The four portraits (and there were probably more in the complete manuscript) are each placed within an elaborately decorated frame; the Virgin and Child (Pl. 4), the portrait of Christ (Pl. 14), if this is really intended as Christ, and the two Evangelists, Matthew and John, are all like icons, with their faces looking out at us with great haunting eyes. There are similar, though much cruder, Evangelist portraits in the Lichfield Gospels and the Gospels at St Gall. There is evidence that the representation of the Virgin is the first in a Western manuscript. Portraits of the Evangelists, however, are found in many manuscripts of the time, and it is normal to portray them holding a book, as do both Matthew (Pl. 11) and John (Pl. 41), or writing with a pen, and it can be seen that John is holding a quill. The very great difference between the portrayal of Matthew and John in Kells and the portrayal of John in Lindisfarne (*f.* 209v) is readily apparent. The former – Kells – style is found particularly in Irish manuscripts, the Book of Dimma, the Book of Mulling, the Stowe Missal, even if much more crudely presented with a far less decorated framework, and in the Irish St Gall Gospels as well as in the Lichfield Gospels. The Lindisfarne style is closely similar to that found in the Italian influenced Codex Amiatinus.

The highly decorated text pages in the Book of Kells are of several kinds. There are the five pages that introduce the text of the Gospels: two in Matthew for the two beginnings (Pls 13 and 19) and one for each beginning of the texts of Mark (Pl. 29), Luke (Pl. 33) and John (Pl. 43). They are by far the most magnificent of the decorated text pages, and the enlargements make it possible to trace the minute detail that goes into their complex and intertwined shapes. All five of them are entirely artistic in intent, with the text on the page subordinated to the design, and some not easily readable even if you know the few words of text to search out.

There are some apparent similarities in treatment between the page beginning Mark and the page beginning John, both having the initial letters IN, but examination of the enlarged details shows how quite different patterns have been used to build up the shapes. The symbol for Matthew appears clearly as the Man in the small panel on the

86

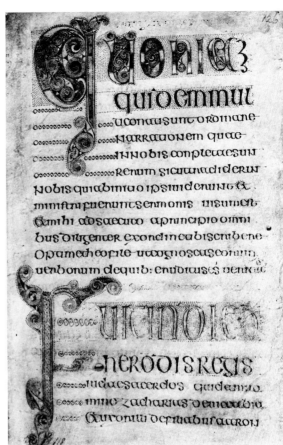

Portrait of St John from the Lindisfarne Gospels (*f.* 209v). British Library

The beginning of Luke from the Book of Durrow (*f.* 126R). Trinity College Library, Dublin

left in Pl. 13, while Mark's symbol of the Lion is entangled with the figure of a man in Pl. 28. The Luke and John pages do not contain their animal symbols. Unlike the other three is the opening page of Luke with its single text word, *Quoniam*. By far the most intricate of these groups of decorated text pages is that for the second beginning in Matthew (Pl. 19), with the highly ornate pattern built around the Greek letters XP, Chi-Rho, to represent the first word, *Christi*. The remaining words, *h (autem) generatio*, appear bleakly at the foot, completely dominated by the network of shapes, faces and animals that cover the whole page. More than any other page in the Book of Kells the Chi-Rho page requires a magnifying glass to separate the minute interweaving of lines

87

The Chi-Rho page from the Lindisfarne Gospels (*f.* 29R). British Library

Beginning of the *Argumentum* of Mark from the Lindisfarne Gospels (*f.* 90R). British Library

throughout the patterns. Three figures of men (or angels), butterflies, a group of cats and mice (or kittens), an upside-down otter holding a fish in its mouth, all of these hide away surrounded by the swirl of confusing geometric patterns. In her section on iconography in the Book of Kells, Mlle Henry points to the symbolism and the wealth of the now lost meanings that surround the animal figures throughout the decoration of the book. The Chi-Rho symbol is found widely as a decoration for these words of the text (i.e. the second beginning of Matthew), sometimes as merely enlarged letters in a page of text, sometimes as in Kells dominating the page.

The similarities and differences of the decoration of Kells, Durrow and Lindisfarne can be seen by comparing the decoration of, first, the words *Liber generationis* (Pl. 13) with the Durrow *Quoniam* (*f.* 126R) and, second, the Chi-Rho pages (Pl. 19 and Lindisfarne *f.* 29R).

On a much smaller scale are the introductory words at the beginning of each of the *Breves causae* and *Argumenta*, where a large decorated initial letter is followed by the remaining letters, often in black, set into vividly coloured bands (Pls 6 and 7). The Lindisfarne Gospels (Lindisfarne *f.* 90R) give them a similar treatment.

Very different from the introductory pages to the Gospels is the decorated introductory text page to the *Breves causae* of Matthew (Pl. 5). Whereas the Gospel

89

introductory pages have only an implied frame not enclosing the page completely (scarcely at all in the Chi-Rho page), Pl. 5 has none of this freedom, for its extensive text is laid out in lines within its decorated framework. The short text of Pl. 37 is also set in a formal, rather crude framework and, similarly, the two *Tunc* pages (Pls 23 and 25), with their fine detail, appear very formal and restrained, though Pl. 24 shows the vividness of the figures within the framework.

Different again are two pages in which, at the dramatic points of the Crucifixion and the Resurrection, the poignant words 'And it was the third hour' (Pl. 30) and 'Now upon the first day of the week' (Pl. 38) stand in decorated ceremonial letters within frames, accompanied by the figures of angels, rather crudely drawn, as are those of men and angels in several of these decorated pages. Among these decorated pages are the pictures of the Arrest (Pl. 22), followed by a page of decorated text (Pl. 23), and the Temptation (Pl. 36), with no text of its own but accompanied by a page of decorated text (Pl. 37).

All these decorated pages form part of the overall plan for the decoration of the book, although it seems certain that we no longer see that plan fully executed, if it ever was completed. One form of decoration that appears in many Insular manuscripts and repeatedly in both the Book of Durrow and the Lindisfarne Gospels is a page entirely covered with an intricate pattern in a symmetrical style, the 'carpet' page. It forms part of the introduction to each of the Gospels in the Book of Durrow and the Lindisfarne Gospels, but in the Book of Kells (Pl. 15) it plays a lesser role, possibly because this style of minute intricate pattern is used so extensively in the other kinds of decorated page. The extraordinary detail of the various patterns of complicated intertwining and geometrical shapes can only be seen properly in the enlargement.

More than any other Insular manuscript, the Book of Kells has a profusion of illustration and ornament, the elements of which are found in other manuscripts but nowhere in such variety. This ornamentation contains many themes: spirals, interlacing, animals and plants both in the large illustrated pages and in the middle of the text. Among the animals we find not only the Man, Lion, Calf and Eagle symbols of the Evangelists, but fish, cats, mice, hens, snakes, dragons and birds of many kinds, sometimes clearly serving as symbols associated with the text, but at others solely as a lively and often humorous decoration. The animals are often intertwined (Pl. 47) and biting each other (Pl. 48) or form part of decorated capitals (Pls 21 and 24).

The spiral is found in the oldest Insular decoration, but in the Book of Kells it is developed into a complicated motif in which one spiral interlaces with another (Pls 15–19). Interlacing is the most frequent form of decoration found in the Insular manuscripts but its profusion and intricacy is remarkable in the Book of Kells, where it not only appears as a framework (Pl. 28) but covers whole panels of decoration, sometimes with animal heads or interweaving limbs (Pls 15 and 43).

The use of plants as decoration in the text is a particular feature of the Book of Kells (Pl. 44). There is no attempt at botanical drawing, just as the animals often bear little resemblance to reality. Both are used as decoration rather than as pictures of actual objects.

The techniques of the painters are many. Clearly, many of their complex patterns are designed with the aid of compasses, but what is most remarkable is the microscopic scale on which the most intricate lines are painted. Frequently it is only in the enlarged details that we can trace the minute forms and shapes that make up a pattern. We know nothing of the implements that they used to achieve this, but they clearly had the finest of pointed brushes, and extraordinary eyesight.

The colours were obtained by pigments dissolved in water with a binding material such as egg-white added. Some of the pigments were minerals: white and red lead, orpiment (for yellow), verdigris (for green), ultramarine (for blue). Others were vegetable or animal extracts: folium (for many shades from blue and pink to purple), indigo or woad (for blue) and kermes (for carmine red). Some of these had to be imported; by far the most expensive was ultramarine from the lapis-lazuli that came from Afghanistan.

The most distinguishing feature of the colouring of the decoration of the Book of Kells is the use of several colours painted one on top of another, giving colour effects also found in the Lichfield Gospels. Like the other Insular manuscripts of the period the painting of the Book of Kells did not make use of gold (it is used just once in the Lindisfarne Gospels).

Mlle Henry has made it clear that the decorations in the Book of Kells represent the work of a group of experts, both scribes and artists working together. However, she does identify three personalities among the painters who did so many different kinds of work: 'the Goldsmith', who produces the effect of metalwork (Pls 13, 15, 19, 29 and 43), the greatest of the craftsmen; 'the Illustrator', a very different person whose interest and expertise lie in the painting of figures (Pls 4, 22 and 36), fond of violent colours and striking washes of purple and green; and 'the Portrait Painter', who produced the striking compositions of Pls 11, 14 and 41.

Although the great paintings are the pages that are the most immediately striking in the manuscript, it is the profusion and variation in the decoration of the text pages that single out the Book of Kells from the other Insular manuscripts. Mlle Henry describes the Book of Kells as the most thoroughly Insular of all Insular manuscripts and as the least representative of the group. Its general trend of decoration conforms with that found in the other manuscripts in the group, but the total effect is more overpowering than that of any other.

V The history of the manuscript

THE FIRST indication of the existence of the manuscript that we call the Book of Kells is in an account, not in Latin but in Irish, of a theft at Kells in the year 1006 (*recte* 1007). The following translation into English is that of Ludwig Bieler.

> The great Gospel of Columkille (Colmcille), the chief relic of the western world, was wickedly stolen during the night from the western sacristy of the great stone church of Cennanus on account of its wrought shrine. That Gospel was found after twenty nights and two months with its gold stolen from it, buried in the ground.

This is the record by the 11th-century annalist copied subsequently into the Annals of Ulster, and it is generally accepted that the annalist's 'great Gospel of Colmcille' is our Book of Kells and that it was from the monastery church of Colmcille at Kells that it was stolen.

A century later, evidence for attributing this manuscript to the Columban monastery at Kells began to be written into some of the blank pages of the manuscript itself. Charters in Irish, recording grants of land to the Church of Colmcille by Irish kings and chiefs, were copied by various hands into the first few blank pages of the Book of Kells in the 12th century. These charters give some indication of the nature of the monastic community at Kells in the 11th and 12th centuries and of the continuation of the ancient Columban organization in which a bishop was a member of the monastery and subject to its head.

By the middle of the 12th century, important changes were taking place at Kells. A new diocese of Kells was established, possibly in 1152, and it seems probable, following the evidence assembled by Professor A. Gwynn, that the ancient monastery church of Colmcille became the cathedral of the diocese. However, the diocese was short-lived and soon after 1211 was absorbed into the diocese of Meath, so that, if it is correct to assume that the Book of Kells passed with the church from the ownership of the Columban monastery of Colmcille to the diocese of Kells in the 12th century, then it is consistent to assume that the book continued to be the property of the same church when it became the parish church of St Columba in the diocese of Kells in the 13th century. If so, the Book of Kells remained at the church through its changes from monastery to parish church. If not, then it would have remained the property of the monastery. We know that the monastery changed from a Columban to an Augustinian community before 1192 and that the abbey was suppressed in 1539 during the Dissolution, its goods and chattels realizing the sum of only £7. 10. 0.

The next writing to be added into the Book of Kells after the 12th-century copying of the Irish charters was two columns of complaint in Latin verse written on the blank page at the end of St Luke's Gospel in the 14th or 15th century. Beneath these are further verses written in the 17th century and signed Richardus Whit, recording in clumsy Latin the famine of 1586, the twelve years of civil war in Queen Elizabeth's reign, the accession of James I in 1602 and the plague in Ireland in 1604, but telling us nothing of the Book of Kells itself nor of St Columba's church.

Scattered through the pages are several insertions which provide glimpses of its history, written not on blank pages but in the text or illustration of the manuscript: on Pls 5, 13, 37 and 43 there are transcriptions in the bottom margin of the Latin ornamental text; Pl. 26 shows an example of the chapter numbers added everywhere, and there are three pages on which, quite shamelessly, notes have been prominently written in English (Pl. 22). Some of these insertions bear the initials G.P. and on f. 334 we find the culprit's name, At the foot of the page stands the note:

I Geralde Plunket of Dublin wrot the contente of every chapter I meane where every chapter doth begyn 1568.

Beneath this is a second note in a different hand, dated but with no name:

the boke contaynes two hondreds V score and iii leves at this present xxvii August 1588.

And then a third note from the next century:

August 24 1621 I reckoned the leaves of this booke and found them to be in number, 344. he who reckoned before me counted six score to the hundred, and. Ja: Ussher Midensis elect:

On the basis of these three notes it was long believed that the Book of Kells became the property of Richard Plunket, the last abbot when the abbey was suppressed in 1539, and that it subsequently passed to our Gerald Plunket, whose identity cannot really be established. It was thought that the manuscript then passed (perhaps through the writer of the second note) to the ownership of James Ussher, Vice Chancellor of the University of Dublin in 1614, Bishop of Meath in 1621 and Archbishop of Armagh in 1625.

James Ussher was one of the earliest students at Trinity College, which was founded in 1592 as the only college of the University of Dublin (as it is even today). As a Fellow of the College he was entrusted with the purchase of books in London for the College Library in 1601 and during the course of this he met Sir Thomas Bodley, one of the greatest of book collectors, who was purchasing books for the University of Oxford. Ussher's interest in manuscripts and books led to his acquiring a large collection of his own, which he took to London when he left Ireland in 1641. His interest in the Book of Kells is reflected not only in his note written on f. 334, but also in his *Britannicarum Ecclesiarum Antiquitates*, published in Dublin in 1639. There he gives a report, first, on the Gospel-Book of Durrow, kept at the monastery of St Columba at Durrow and reputed to have been dictated by Columba himself; and, second, on the no less ancient book held sacred by the men of Meath in the town of Kells. Ussher states that he has collated both books with the text of the Vulgate.

There is no evidence that Ussher ever owned the Book of Kells and there are several clear indications that it was not among his possessions. The extraordinary account of Ussher's great collections of manuscripts and books, and how eventually they came to the Library of Trinity College in 1661, cannot therefore any longer be considered as part of the history of the Book of Kells.

Before we come to the manuscript's arrival in the College Library, there is a further reference to the Book of Kells in a report made in 1665 for the Down Survey. This tells us (with modernized spelling as given by Professor Gwynn):

> The chief town of this barony is Kells. . . . Here is also a large church, but ruinous: one end is covered, wherein the horses quarter that are in garrison there . . . on the northwest side thereof stands a little house. . . . This house, they say, was the cell of Columkill, one of the chief patrons of Ireland. . . . The inhabitants of this town have for many hundred years past had the keeping of a large parchment manuscript in Irish, written as they say by Columkill's own hand, but of such a character that none of this age can read it. The said writing was about a year and a half ago sent to the late commissioners of the commonwealth by the governor of Kells.

It is clear that the surveyor and presumably most of the inhabitants knew nothing of the great past of the monastery or its famous Gospel-Book, which the surveyor believed to be written in Irish.

It is strange that the circumstances surrounding the gift of the Book of Kells to Trinity College Library were forgotten, while the donor of the Book of Durrow to the Library, Henry Jones, was well remembered. This Henry Jones was appointed Vice-Chancellor of the University of Dublin in 1646 and was Scoutmaster-general to Cromwell's army in Ireland. He became Bishop of Meath in 1661. It is now clear from the statement in a letter of 19 April 1681, whose significance as the missing clue was identified by Mr W. O'Sullivan, present Keeper of Manuscripts in the Library, that this same Henry Jones was also the donor of the Book of Kells. The letter is from William Pallister of Trinity College, himself one of the Library's benefactors, and relates how he had been assured by the Bishop of Meath that:

> S. Columkill's and the Cupboard MS were those mentioned by the primate [James Ussher] in his de Primord, p. 691 [*Britannicarum Ecclesiarum Antiquitates*], there judged of equal antiquity, and that himself was assistant to the primate in collating them, and bestowed both upon our library.

The Cupboard MS can be identified as the Book of Durrow. Our Book of Kells is St Columkill's MS.

For a long time after its arrival in the College Library the Book of Kells was not always treated with sufficient care. It was bound and rebound several times, disastrously so in the 18th century, when the pages were trimmed by a bookbinder. Some margins appear to have lost almost an inch and a few of the illustrated pages were damaged by this means.

Time has given the Book of Kells both losses and gains (or at least regains). Today the four volumes contain 340 folios. Ussher counted 344 in the year 1621, but the manuscript should have had 370 folios if it was properly completed some twelve hundred years ago. Two further notes are to be found, written in near the end of the manuscript at the top of *f.* 337R. First:

here lacketh a leafe being y beginnyng of y xvi chapt. of St John,

and then:

this leaf found 1741.

Even in the early 19th century, the Book of Kells had not achieved the fame that it has held since, and it was possible for both Gospel-Books, Kells and Durrow, to be mislaid in the College Library when a list of twelve early Irish manuscripts was compiled in 1814, although the Book of Durrow was found in time for it to be included in an appendix to the list. The Book of Kells was found in the Library shortly afterwards.

The last rebinding in the 19th century was in 1895. It did not last long and some folios were loose by the time it was decided that a more drastic treatment was needed to preserve the manuscript for the future. In 1953 a major process of restoration and binding was carried out by Mr Roger Powell, and the Book of Kells was bound into four volumes with an expertise that should ensure that the manuscript will survive without deterioration long into the future, provided it is given the right conditions. In the Long Room (the Library building of 1732), two volumes of the Book of Kells are daily on display, with the volumes and the pages at which they are opened changed on a regular basis. Both in their display cases and in storage the volumes are kept in strictly controlled conditions to prevent damage or deterioration. The preservation of all medieval manuscripts requires very strict conservation measures. For the Book of Kells, one of the greatest treasures to have survived from medieval Europe, these measures have to be extreme to compensate for the hardships the manuscript has had to bear in the past and to ensure that it survives for future generations in the condition in which we have inherited it.

Reading list

The brief text that accompanies these reproductions from the Book of Kells provides only a summary view of the background from which the manuscript had its origin and of the manuscript's most outstanding features. A much more detailed treatment of these topics will be found in the books listed here for further reading and through the bibliographies and references that they contain.

A complete facsimile of the Book of Kells was published thirty years ago in three volumes, with an introduction by E. H. Alton, Peter Meyer and G. O. Simms:

Evangeliorum quattuor Codex Cenannensis. Urs Graf, Bern 1950.

An extensive selection of pages from the Book of Kells reproduced in colour with enlargements of details was published six years ago, with a study of the manuscript by Françoise Henry:

The Book of Kells. Thames and Hudson, London 1974.

Both of these are invaluable for more detailed study of the text, the script and the decoration.

THE CONTINENTAL BACKGROUND

E. R. Curtius *European Literature and the Latin Middle Ages.* Translated by W. R. Trask. Routledge & Kegan Paul, London 1953

W. P. Ker *The Dark Ages* (reissued) Nelson, London 1955

R. A. B. Mynors, editor *Cassiodori Senatoris Institutiones.* Oxford University Press, Oxford 1937

THE ISLAND TRADITIONS

B. Colgrave & R. A. B. Mynors, editors Bede's *Ecclesiastical History of the English People.* Clarendon Press, Oxford 1969

F. M. Stenton *Anglo-Saxon England,* 3rd edition. Clarendon Press, Oxford 1971

Máire and Liam de Paor *Early Christian Ireland.* Thames and Hudson, London 1958

L. Bieler *Ireland Harbinger of the Middle Ages.* Oxford University Press, London 1963

THE SCRIBES AND THEIR TEXTS

T. J. Brown 'Northumbria and the Book of Kells', in: *Anglo-Saxon England I.* Edited by Peter Clemoes, pp. 219–46. Cambridge University Press, Cambridge 1972

J. Wordsworth & H. J. White *Novum Testamentum ... Latine, secundum editionem Sancti Hieronymi.* Clarendon Press, Oxford 1889–1954

THE ILLUMINATION

F. Henry *Irish Art in the Early Christian Period (to AD 800).* Revised edition. Methuen, London 1965

F. Henry *Irish Art during the Viking invasions.* Methuen, London 1967

A Grabar *Early Medieval Painting from the fourth to the eleventh century* (Book illumination by Carl Nordenfalk). Skira, New York 1957

THE HISTORY OF THE MANUSCRIPT

Sir Edward Sullivan *The Book of Kells* (Fifth edition). Studio Publications, London 1952

A. Gwynn 'Some notes on the history of the Book of Kells', in: *Irish Historical Studies.* Vol IX, no. 34, 1954, pp. 129–61

The subsequent note by Mr W. O'Sullivan on the donor appeared in Vol. XI, no. 41, 1958, pp. 5–7